Manners on the Move

from the *Sandbox*

to the *Executive Suite*

Etiquette and Communication nuggets for everyday occasions

Dr. Janet T. Cherry
Judith A. Burda

Thank You

to everyone who contributed
to make this book a reality!

A special thanks to David J. Kreher,
Attorney at Law, for his help with legal matters
and
Anna McNeill for her marketing advice.

FOREWORD

"When 'less' is never 'more'."

With the emphasis on nutrition today, many products promoting fewer calories will often state that "less is more." While this might work for nutrition, it does not work for the major "life" category of manners. The digital society and an informal cultural influence have lessened our attention to manners today to a point that many simply do not know or appreciate the use of manners, particularly as it relates to one's image or personal brand.

In working with future career professionals, I have found that this topic is as important as any academic topic they pursue. Whether the focus is on writing an appropriate thank you or cover letter, responding to an invitation, eating a meal with appropriate poise and polish, or simply using the important words, "please and thank you," these former "life lessons" are critical to one's personal and professional success.

How did our culture move toward such a low awareness of the importance of manners? Certainly, earlier generations recognized appropriate dress requirements for events, ordering protocol in a restaurant, or communication expectations in daily interchange. How is it that as advanced as we are in technology, science, and electronic communication, we are lacking in this important area of personal polish and excellence?

You probably have your own perceptions of this occurrence but hopefully you will agree that we need to rectify this gap and move toward a more mannerly environment, at home, in the office, at school, and yes, even in public. Why is this change so important? The absence of manners in one's personal brand speaks volumes as they interact and the importance of a polished image makes a difference in many interactions which can impact career opportunities and personal successes.

I encourage you to read this book with careful consideration—how can you share these nuggets of etiquette wisdom? Will your colleagues benefit? Do you know "professionals of tomorrow" who would find value in the pages to come? Would your family members find a few reminders helpful?

Dr. Janet Cherry has been a coach and advocate of mannerly behavior for many years. Her passion to help others in this area is impressive and contagious. I believe once you read this book, you'll find something that you will also be reminded of or introduced to for use in your own personal and professional spaces.

Enjoy this book, but more importantly **share this book** with those you know will not only value but use its treasures of wisdom.

Here's to a polished and professional future generation!

Kathy Tuberville, SPHR, Ed.D.
George Johnson Fellow
Ron Hart Leader
Department of Management
Director, Avron B. Fogelman Professional Development Center
Fogelman College of Business and Economics
The University of Memphis
Memphis, Tennessee

Welcome to

Manners on the Move

Manners make every move with us—the good and the not-so-good—from the sandbox to the executive suite. These communication and etiquette nuggets are a quick polish for life's everyday occasions: workplace, formal and casual dining, public places, school, and at home to name a few.

My professional career—as a corporate trainer, university communications instructor, professional speaker, small business owner, certified etiquette coach, and radio talk show host—gives me the insight for this book. Listening and manners, both my passions, are communication-based. From my radio show guests, I collected expert advice on acceptable manners for everyday occasions. These professionals witness "manners in motion" every single day. In *Manners on the Move*, they graciously share their thoughts and advice for making you a class act.

It is said a picture is worth a thousand words. I have certainly written well over a thousand words. The light-hearted pictures give them life. I teamed up with Judy Burda, a graphic artist extraordinaire. She is creative, technical, and a five-star professional. Chemistry clicks between the graphics and the words throughout this book.

If respect is genuine, a faux pas is easily forgiven. If you are unsure of an acceptable behavior or verbal exchange, spend time with the wonderful guests who made this book possible. You can be a shining star for an immediate occasion and for a lifetime.

Enjoy!

Dr. Janet T. Cherry

Although there are tips in every topic for everyone, we have used the following code to help with emphasis on certain groups.

CODE:
C=CHILDREN
F=FAMILY
P=PROFESSIONAL

As we know, a picture is worth a thousand words; hence, we have the pictures to go with the words.

Study the Table of Contents,
   Skim the entire book,
      Devour the pages, lists, and pictures for your occasions.

For quick reference when you are on the go, take the On-The-Go Tips cards (pages 192-194) with you.

We want you to be a shining star at your special event and situation!

Janet & Judy

TABLE OF CONTENTS

(C,F,P)   Manners from the Sandbox to the
Executive Suite 10

(F,P)   Where Do Manners Come From? 13

(F,P)   A Gentleman Is…? 17

(F,P)   A Lady Is…? 21

(C,F,P)   And Your RSVP 24

(C,F,P)   Thank You 25

(C,F,P)   If it is Raining and If it is Snowing 31

(C,F,P)   With Your Cell Phone 32

(C,F,P)   In the Place of Worship of Your Choice 34

(C,F,P)   First Impressions 35

(C,F,P)   With Quiz #1 38

(F,P)   ?Questioning? 39

(F,P)   Communicating Assertively and Respectfully 43

(C,F,P)   Manners in Conversation 47

(C,F,P)   Kindness 51

          On-the-Go Tips Card 193

(C,F,P)   Listening 55

(P)   Workplace Manners and
Internal Communications 61

(P)   When Preparing for and Attending Meetings 66

(P)   The Interview 67

(C,F,P)   In the Hospital or Visiting the Sick 74

(P)   Dress for Success 75

(C,F,P)   With Four Steps to a Proper Handshake 79

          On-the-Go Tips Card 193

(C,F,P)   Formal Dining Picture 80

(C,F,P)   Formal Dining Faux Pas 82

(C,F,P)   Formal Dining Table Setting 83

          On-the-Go Tips Card 193

(C,F,P)   With Quiz #2 89

(C,F,P)   The Flag of The United States of America 90

(F,P)   Wine and Roses 91

(F,P)   Pet Peeves of Restaurant Servers 95

(F,P)	Guest Services in the Hospitality Industry	99
(C,F,P)	Manners for Roommates	103
(C,F,P)	In the Grocery and Other Retail Stores	108
(F,P)	Manners for the Gay Community	109
(C,F,P)	On Elevators and on Escalators	114
(C,F,P)	Dog and Puppy Manners	115
(C,F)	At the Zoo	120
(C,F,P)	At Fast Food Restaurants	122
(C,F)	School Manners	123
(C,F,P)	With Quiz #3	128
(C,F,P)	In Theatres and in Movies	129
(C,F,P)	At the Fitness Center/Gym	130
(C,F,P)	Sports Manners	131
(C,F,P)	In Public Restrooms	134
(C,F,P)	Condominium Living	135
(C,F,P)	On Sidewalks and in the Streets!	140
(F,P)	Funeral Manners	141
(F,P)	Pop-Up Events	145
(P)	Sales Manners	149
(F,P)	Driving Manners	153
(C,F,P)	At the Buffet	158
(F,P)	The Break-Up	159
(C,F,P)	In Languages	164
	On-the-Go Tips Card	193
(F,P)	Checklist for International Travel	165
(F,P)	Cuba Travel	171
(C,F,P)	On Public Transportation	176
(F,P)	Travel to Israel	177
(P)	With Your Business Cards	182
(F,P)	Latin American Travel	183
	On-The-Go Tips Cards Information	192
	Guest Index	199

MANNERS: FROM THE SANDBOX TO THE EXECUTIVE SUITE

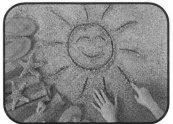

"Play is the beginning of knowledge."
--George Washington Emery Dorsey

What I most remember about the sandbox is having to put on my little sun bonnet before I could go out the door. I loved to play with my sand toys. Since moving to my latest "executive suite" (actually my desk in the kitchen) and reflecting on my days in the sandbox, I find many of the same "rules" still apply.

The sandbox is a great place to practice good manners.

Invite one or more friends to join you in the sandbox. Although it can be fun to play by yourself, it is also fun to spend time playing with others.

Share your tools without being told to share.

Help your friends make a sand castle if this is their first time in the sandbox.

Learn from the ideas your friends bring to your play session. I have heard it said that two heads are often better than one.

Keep sand away from your eyes and your friends' eyes. Sand in your eyes can really hurt and the sting takes the fun away.

Make a lot of different things and then decide which one is your favorite.

🐾 Keep at it until you get it just the way you imagined it should be.

🐾 Tell your friends how much you like what they have made.

🐾 Thank them for coming to visit and joining you in your sandbox.

🐾 Keep the memories of that special time. They just might come in handy one day.

And before you know it, you have moved into your very own executive suite. This might seem strange and new at first, just like the new sandbox when it was delivered. Yet, as you look around, you find it reminds you of the days you and your friends had fun playing and making all sorts of things, even sand castles where dreams and magic often live.

The executive suite is a great place to put into practice some of the things you learned in your sandbox many years ago.

🐾 Invite the members of your team to join you for a brain storming session.

🐾 Share your experience and knowledge—your tools.

🐾 Help your team to grow while reaching positive outcomes.

🐾 Appreciate the ideas your team brings to the table. Two sets of eyes can see the advantages in setting up a design in different ways.

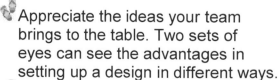

🐾 Keep negative comments away from your conversation.

♪ Negativism can stun creativity.

♪ Visit the plus and minus of everything offered as a possible solution.

♪ Keep at it until you get it just the way you imagined it should be.

♪ Tell your team how important their ideas have been in finding a solution.

♪ Thank them for being a member of your team.

♪ Keep the results of that special session and build on it. Teamwork fosters success and success will grow.

Sometimes we are in a hurry and we forget what stage of learning and growing we have achieved. Taking life one day at a time and remembering that life in the "executive suite" can be just as much fun as playing in the sandbox. It is all in the way we look at the "castle" and the people who "play and build" with us.

Enjoy! Remember your manners follow you wherever you go.

Dr. Janet T. Cherry, *Author*

12

WHERE DO MANNERS COME FROM...
WHERE WILL MANNERS TAKE YOU?

"Nothing opens doors like good manners."
--A. McNeill

To be specific, most of the practices we term as "manners" today actually stem from behaviors in the past formed to protect, preserve, predict, entertain, or befriend. These practices were passed down through the years, modified in some regard, and exist today to show respect for ourselves and the people and creatures in the world around us.

For example, the blade of the knife faces in and toward your plate when setting the table because Knights would only place the blade out if someone were to be killed during dinner. Today, we just follow practice for the blade to be "in" rather than "out."

The literal meaning of this conversation's question was intending a pause for thought on where WE, as a nation's people, "get manners." Our conversation attempts to provide suggestions. Take a hint from this book's cover as to where manners may take you—from the sandbox to the executive suite.

My guest was Dr. Barbara Davis, faculty at The University of Memphis, Memphis, Tennessee. I have known and worked with Barbara on communication and etiquette projects through the years. Her thoughts and comments about where our manners come from and where they take us are below.

🦶 Foremost, manners are introduced and practiced within the family and at home.

🦶 Our family becomes our primary role models. Good manners become a habit from childhood and grow with us until we then become the teacher. Training in respect and positive behaviors should be encouraged from a very young age.

🦶 Life is a journey. It seems the journey is moving faster and faster. Manners are a part of us and move with us. Success and happiness most always go hand in hand with good manners—showing respect for yourself and others.

🦶 We all learn quicker when there is a "why" explanation to go along with the lesson. Compliments and appreciation for correct practice seem to stick with us and foster turning practice into a habit.

🦶 Hundreds of books on etiquette and manners are readily available from libraries to downloads and from Google and Amazon to apps covering hundreds more topics and situations.

- The *Manners Always Matter* radio talk show, Janet hosted, was conceived and aired to provide listeners with yet another source of information and polish to shine our image.

- Media and talk shows are increasingly devoting time and topic to the apparent lack of manners in today's world and begging the question, "What has happened to manners—where have they gone?"

Today's casual attitude is becoming more accepted and widespread. We need to remember that good manners speak loudly and in volumes about YOU and WHO you represent. When you show up, your manners—shiny or dull—show up with you.

Good manners are a plus on playgrounds, in sports, in the classroom (from kindergarten to university), on the job, and in the community. Good manners (as will not-so-good manners) set you apart as a job applicant, volunteer, corporate leader, or government representative.

Universities, such as The University of Memphis, are establishing programs to promote the development and polish needed to round out student academic skills and prepare graduates for competitive excellence.

- The University of Memphis includes preparation in résumé writing and interview practice, follow-up courtesies, professional attire, instruction for social functions, and formal dining  etiquette. Many students do not fully appreciate what they don't know until after attending these programs.

- Preparation for any function is more than a last-minute thought. Student feedback is extremely positive for our Professional Development program series.

Globalization, a diverse workforce, technology, teamwork, and ethical issues all heavily influence business environments today. Exhibiting common rules of basic etiquette ensures a more enjoyable, productive, and safe workplace for everyone.

I'm sure you have heard quotes that most of success is showing up.

I follow with a quote from Dianna Booher,

"Be present when you show up."

She suggests showing up on time, being accountable, being prepared, and being involved. I agree and add:

"Be sure you also show up with good manners!"

Dr. Barbara D. Davis, *an Associate Professor of Management in Fogelman College of Business at The University of Memphis, is an etiquette consultant and coordinates the Etiquette Program at The UofM. Dr. Davis teaches Business and Intercultural Communication courses and recently received the 2016 Excellence in Teaching Award from the Black Scholars Organization.*

A GENTLEMAN IS...?

"Being male is a matter of birth;
being a man is a matter of age;
but, being a gentleman is a matter of choice."
--Author Unknown

A gentleman is a gentleman for all times—not just "when on display." What constitutes a "gentleman" in the eyes of a female? What are her expectations? My guest for this conversation was Jim Frommel, a *gentleman* I have known and worked with as a volunteer for over 10 years. He and I thought it would be enlightening to pose this question to females, unknown to us except by age and answer. We asked 47 females in three age groups: 18-35, 36-55, 56+ questions about *dining, social settings,* and *grooming.*

One specific question was asked of all 47: To be a gentleman, should age matter?

Their unanimous answer was
"No."

The most frequent additional comment: Remembering to call, email, or text saying you enjoyed being with me—or even just one word, "Hi." Bringing a "favorite something" for no reason (a single favorite flower or vegetable from your garden, a decadent treat, a clipping from a paper/magazine, or a book).

These are symbols from the heart letting the lady know you respect her and share thoughts of her after you parted.

I have often felt this goes a long way toward making up for an etiquette mistake or two. Remember, the most appreciated is often the most unexpected.

When I am *dining* with a gentleman, I expect him to:

- Use dining utensils and napkin appropriately; no elbows on the table. (41)

- Not talk about work, dead wives, ex-girlfriends—find out more about me. (36)

- Not spend all his time on the cell phone. (31)

- Not eat so fast I am left eating alone. (25)

- Not stuff his mouth too full of food and then talk. (21)

This list reminded me—and I admit—of being a fast eater. I am slowing down. One suggestion I read suggested to pause and really listen to my companion during the meal—this works!

I also know that my companion should order her own meal. The day has passed when the man orders for both. One statement I was surprised not to see is about who pays and tips. If the man extended the invitation, he pays—no question.

When I am with a gentleman in a *social* setting, I expect him to:

Dress appropriately for the occasion and advise me. (46)

Be ready to leave when it is time to go. (46)

Introduce me to people, especially the host/hostess and include me in conversations. (43)

Treat me with respect in all situations. (37)

Thank the host/hostess before leaving. (36)

Of the items mentioned in this category, I feel the most important is making sure the person I have invited feels comfortable. Be sure she is introduced to the host/hostess if she does not know them, and introduce her to others there I may know. She is my guest.

I expect a gentleman's *dress* and *grooming* to:

Smell fresh and appealing—but not "loud." (44)

Have pants that don't have to be held up to stay up. (41)

Have polished shoes and over the calf socks. (37)

Have clean and pressed clothes that fit. (36)

Have a neat haircut and neatly trimmed and clean fingernails. (25)

My grandfather, a salesman, was always noticed for the way he dressed. What impressed me most about his dress were his shoes and socks—always shined shoes and socks never showing his leg. To this day, he is my role model and a constant reminder of appropriate appearance and dress.

Jim Frommel *retired as director of business affairs at WMC TV/AM/FM; later working in the financial services field as a planner and advisor. He is a volunteer with SCORE as a mentor/counselor to small business owners, and also as a board member at Theatre Memphis.*

A LADY IS...?

We are who we are every single day of our lives. Many eyes may see us differently and that is OK, just so we know whose reflection is in the mirror.

What constitutes a "lady" in the eyes of a male? What are his expectations? Our survey responses appear below. There was no guest. In fact, "A Lady Is...?" did not air. This is one of a few where Saturday morning show time ran out too soon. However, I wanted to include it for balance.

The same survey was distributed as for "A Gentleman Is...?" I found the results very interesting. I hope you will, too. Just goes to show how similar and yet how different a lady's and a gentleman's expectations can be. We asked 35 men in three age groups: 18-35, 36-55, 56+ the same questions about *dining, social settings, and grooming.*

One specific question was asked of all 35: *To be a lady, should age matter?*

Their unanimous answer was "**No**."

When asked what comes to mind when you think/hear the word "lady" among the most frequent words listed were: caring, kind, proud, charming, and magical (can fix anything). Some respondents also answered with mother, grandmother, and wife.

21

Another stream of responses that came through saw the lady as a "peacemaker"—a person who quietly holds the family or group together.

The comments as listed ranked highest of all three age categories. When I am *dining* with a lady, I expect her to:

- Have good table and eating manners. (28)
- Know what she wants to eat and enjoys it. (25)
- Be pleasant and friendly to everyone. (19)
- Not talk on the phone—talk to me. (15)
- Keep conversation happy and not talk about problems or things that need fixing or talk about other people while having dinner. (11)

The comment about talking on the phone was a bit of a surprise since it is so common to see both men and women, seated together, talking on their cell phones when dining in a restaurant.

When I am with a lady in a *social* setting, I expect her to:

- Talk to people and act friendly. (24)
- Know how to look, dress, and act. (23)
- Stay near me and behave as if she enjoys being with me. (21)
- Enjoy herself. (18)
- Eat correctly if there is food. (12)

Of the items mentioned in this category, all age groups, the responses indicated significant importance to having a companion show she enjoyed the person she is with and will express it.

I expect a lady's *dress* and *grooming* to:

- Be appropriate for her age. (29)
- Smell inviting and fresh. (22)
- Look comfortable. (16)
- Not have hair in her eyes nor play with her hair. (14)
- Not have fingernails that stab you. (10)

As a whole, gentlemen like for their lady to give them attention and look and act in a way they will be proud to have her on their arm. If you look back at the Gentleman's responses, the ladies wanted their gentlemen to be with them and follow-up after a time spent together with a thoughtful call or email.

In his blog, *In pursuit of Elegance,* Matthew E. May, defines elegance as "Something that is two things at once: unusually simple and surprisingly powerful. One without the other leaves you short of elegance." I see a lady in this definition— she is seldom overstated or loud, yet when an occasion calls for it, she has the strength and presence to rise to the occasion.

Although listening showed up directly in only one response, a good listener goes hand in hand with the total impression expressed by both male and female. Listening is the highest compliment you can extend to another and it usually places very high on most manners' lists. Don't forget to include it.

Dr. Janet T. Cherry, Author

Don't Forget Your Manners!
…And Your RSVP

🩴 RSVP is French for Réspondez,
s'il vous plaît, which in English means, "please respond."
(It does NOT mean Refreshments Served Very Promptly.)

🩴 Respond to every invitation by the stated date.

🩴 Reply as stated: mail, telephone, or email.

🩴 Follow the information provided. "Reply: regrets only." You
only need to reply if *unable* to attend a function.

🩴 Reply only for people who *were* invited. Follow the
wording on the envelope. If only your name appears, you
should *not* bring a guest and only reply for yourself. If the
envelope states, your name and a guest, then your reply
should include your name
and a guest's name.

🩴 Look at the RSVP card, if
provided. If there is an "M"
followed by a line printed
on the card, the "M" stands
for the first letter of the *title*

of the person attending (Mr., Mrs., Ms.) followed by the
name. If the title is Dr., Judge, Rev., or something other,
simply write the appropriate title. Do not cross out the "M"
just ignore it. If you are having cards printed, omit the "M"
and have lines reading, "names of those attending."

🩴 RSVP … to provide planning considerations to the
host/hostess for space, food, name tags, take-aways, and
peace of mind in feeling there will be
fewer surprises when the door is
opened to welcome guests or when
guests gather around the table and
there are not enough chairs or
chicken!

24

THANK YOU

"My heart is bursting with thanks for your part in this journey."
--Dr. Janet T. Cherry

This book is based on the 52 radio shows hosted on Station KWAM 990 AM Talk Radio in Memphis, Tennessee. What a challenge. What fun. What a learning experience. The first program aired in January and the last in December. Because they aired in a major gift-giving season, they both featured the importance of *Thank You—spoken and written.* Expressing thanks is one of my passions. The other is listening—both communications are based on acts of manners.

My guest for the first program was Judy Burda, the co-author of this book. My guest on the last show was Anthony Holmes, my producer. The messages were much the same—when, how, and what to say. We talked about many things, shared resources, and said thanks to a lot of people. The tips below are from the combined broadcasts, answering many of the questions often asked of listeners and workshop participants.

Manners display *RESPECT* for yourself and one another.

Showing respect allows others to become comfortable and feel valued in every situation.

The *Magic Words,* learned when we are young, and used throughout life, are the starting point. They are not just used in specific geographic locations—they are universal:

Please: Gives any request a softer more genuine sound. Asking another individual to complete a task or stop a behavior or assist with an activity will sound less like a command and more of an appeal when introduced with the word, *"please."*

Thank You*:* In every single day, we are blessed with so many words and acts of kindness there is never a shortage of reasons to say or express our thanks. Thanks may come in a personal conversation, an email, a phone call, or in a written thank you card or letter. The personal touch of the thank you note is most appreciated because of the special attention it requires. Expressing thanks should become a habit. Just a few words from your heart may do wonders for the receiver's heart.

You're Welcome*:* Time is our most precious gift. When we invest our time to bring happiness and comfort to another it is only fitting to receive appreciation. We acknowledge appreciation by genuinely letting the person know we were happy to be able to help. All our *magic words* must be perceived as being from the heart. Your tone of voice and body language confirm it.

Excuse Me: No one of us is perfect. There are times when we mess up. We must be confident enough in ourselves to acknowledge our error. Saying *"excuse me"* or *"I'm sorry"* is a first step in moving past our mistakes. Let someone know our behaviors did not intend to offend and we ask for the opportunity to make amends and move forward.

When to begin…We shared agreement that children can begin to learn manners at a very young age. Toddlers in the sandbox, in a kiddie pool, or on the playground all have occasions to share and use the magic words. (You might want to read the chapter on Manners from the Sandbox to the Executive Suite.)

 Thank you notes also can begin at a young age. One example offered, with permission to use in the book, is from Phyllis Gregory and her daughter, Ella. Phyllis started coaching Ella when she was around three years of age. The cards started with colorful crayon drawings, finished with a note from Phyllis regarding the gift. As Ella learned, she would print her name. Later, Ella wrote and signed— but still included drawings. The gifts were expressed in the drawings. A delight to receive. This began with mother and daughter preparing their cards. Role modeling and motivation were in place.

On the way to growing up and becoming an independent writer, another suggestion for the young crowd is to design a card with a mixture of words and blank lines for fill-in-the-blanks—an age up—yet still simple.

 When to end…Never!

Why are Thank You cards and messages sent? Thank you cards and messages are sent for a variety of reasons:

- Gift acknowledgment—even if you have already said thanks in person.

- For the hospitality of a host/hostess for overnight stays, dinners, and other occasions.

- For any special treat or favor received (helping you through a difficult time, sharing a skill, assisting you when you are ill, and flowers, as examples).

How and when do you send a Thank You message?

Tradition recommends a small note card, approximately 4" x 5" folded, handwritten and addressed, and mailed. There are all kinds of cards available: packaged, printed, engraved, and created. Cards can range from expensive to inexpensive. The dollar stores have packaged and loose cards from $0.50 to $1.00. Let us emphasize, it is not the cost of the card, it is the sentiment and the words expressed in the card that make the difference.

- Today's world accepts the practice of email messages for *informal* situations. Texting is just ahead of nothing. The handwritten card is still preferred. Business letters may also be appropriate in the corporate and professional arena, particularly in the case of a follow-up to an employment interview.

- Telephone calls are also acceptable for an expression of thanks. There are times when a call is a better choice—if the person is home bound, a call and phone visit may be very welcome. A one-on-one thank you is also acceptable. However, it is followed by a written note.

What do you say in a Thank You message?

- Make your message timely. Don't wait so long that a person forgets what they did, why, and for whom.

- Select a delivery system to match the occasion.

- Select an appropriate card or stationery. Some people do not feel the card should say "Thank You." We see no problem with that. After all, Happy Birthday, Get Well, Sympathy, as examples, all are stated on the front of cards.

- Start with a salutation, "Dear Karen," for instance.

- Begin the note with words other than "Thank you."

- State the reason for the note. (The flowers from your garden are lovely. Thank you for sharing. I am enjoying them. Or, The yellow sweater is perfect. I will enjoy wearing it.)

- Include something about the person you are writing. (Enjoy your trip next week.)

- End your note with an appropriate close. (Sincerely or Fondly, as examples.)

- Sign your name.

- Date the note at the bottom.

- The envelope should also be handwritten. All names should have a title (Mr., Mrs., Ms., Doctor, etc.). The full address, city, two letter state abbreviation, and zip code. The return address, since the envelope is small, is placed on the back of the envelope. Don't forget the stamp.

The message need not be long—two to four sentences— just warm and sincere. The formality of the note depends on how well you know the recipient.

The important message here is *to do it* and do it in a *prompt manner.* When a person invests time and money in selecting and sending a gift, that person wants to know the gift arrived and was received as intended.

 We have heard stories where a thank you was not sent at all or sent months after when the giver did not even remember sending a gift. In college classrooms, you will find students who have never sent a thank you card—that's entirely too late!

If you are stuck on card selection, or suggestions for what to say, the Hallmark website, *http://ideas.hallmark.com/articles/thank-you-ideas/thank-you-messages-what-to-write-in-a-thank-you-card* is an excellent resource.

Sending a thank you note, or other messages of appreciation and gratitude, is a habit worth forming. Not only does it make you feel good, it makes someone else feel special.

Dr. Janet T. Cherry and *Judith A. Burda*
Co-Authors

Anthony "Dulaa" Holmes has gained the respect of many in the music industry as an artist, composer, and producer. He is the owner of the Memphis-based recording studio, Reality Records. Dulaa founded the UCanB Movement, offering Memphis youth an opportunity to explore their musical talent and live a positive lifestyle.

Don't Forget Your Manners!
...If it is Raining

Open your umbrella *after* you are completely outside and beyond the door.

Shake and close the umbrella, with your back to the door, before entering a transportation vehicle or a building.

Hold an open umbrella high enough not to block vision.

Hold a closed umbrella straight down so as not to give anyone an unintentional tickle.

Please don't splash in a puddle!

...And, if it is Snowing

Hold the temptation to fire off a snowball until you reach a wide-open area.

(Then, go for it; have fun!)

Be careful!

Don't Forget Your Manners!
…With Your Cell Phone

 Read these numbers from the Pew Research Center: *90% of American adults own a cell phone.* Cherry and Burda, *Manners on the Move*, feel at least 89% of American adults (plus the kids) who own cell phones need better manners to go with their phones!

Check your speaking voice. There is no need to speak louder on a cell phone— even on international calls. You can also use a cell phone without pacing.

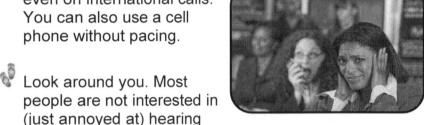

Look around you. Most people are not interested in (just annoyed at) hearing your conversation. Yet, you never know WHO *is* listening or what they ***do*** with the information they hear.

Remember, to date, no public place has been designated as a cell phone center: waiting rooms, public transportation, restaurants, movies, etc.

 Talk to your restaurant server and the person who accompanied you to dinner. The server is busy; your guest is bored.

- Set an example by not having your cell phone on the dinner table. *(The answer to the question on the book's back cover: There is NO place designated for cell phones on the dinner table—casual or formal.)*

- Honor announcements stating (or have the good sense to already know) meetings, social events, church, funerals, weddings, sporting events, etc., are "unplugged" events.

- Give priority to those in front of you. Put the phone away.

- Never use a cell phone while driving! This is a "No. 1 No, Never." **It *is* dangerous; it *can* be deadly.**

- *Enjoy technology. It has its place—as do good manners!*

Don't Forget Your Manners!

...In the Place of Worship of
Your Choice

 Focus on why you are there.

Dress respectfully for entering a house of worship. The following examples go for men, women, and teens. Shorts, slogan T-shirts, shirts not designed to be worn untucked, halter-top, bare-back, or strapless dresses do not have a place in church. (Test: would you wear your intended attire to a job interview, to work, or to a formal dinner party? If your answer is "no" then rethink your clothing choice before leaving your home.)

Control children. This is a teaching moment—be a positive role model. Children should not be allowed to roam the aisles, bang on pews, or annoy the people in the pews around them. Parents, fix your child's hair at home. Let's teach them to sit, stand, or kneel as appropriate.

Role Models: refrain from checking and using YOUR cell phone during the service. Another teaching and role model opportunity. Place your cell phone on vibrate if you are expecting an emergency call. Better yet, leave it in the car or at home.

Stay until the officiating clergy have left the pulpit or altar and are outside of the sanctuary—and to show respect, stay in place until the music ends. Avoid running over people to exit quickly. If doors are involved, always look behind you to see that you are not allowing a door to close in someone's face nor an umbrella to pop up in their face.

Show respect and courtesy for others leaving the service when exiting the parking lot. It takes only a minute to display a friendly smile on both sides of the church doors.

FIRST IMPRESSIONS

"Make the most of yourself,
for that is all there is of you."
--Ralph Waldo Emerson

Can you name five things you can do in one minute or less? Take a minute to think about it—jot your answers down.

Time's up! Did you get five things written down?

You can…send a short email, or give your dog a bone, or put on your socks, or address an envelope…or…

You can make a first impression.

What exactly is meant by a "first impression?" The body movements we make, the sound of our voice, the words we speak, the style of our walk, the clothes we choose, the facial expressions we show—all rolled up together are a profile of ourselves for others to observe. Most are also a reflection of good manners. How many of these behaviors are involved in making a person feel comfortable? How many, if not delivered in a positive way, reveal our own lack of comfort when dealing with others? Some of them—the handshake for one—also reveal cultural etiquette. In total, this is a person's "first impression" of us. Any one of the mannerisms listed below can label the first impression as unfavorable.

- Shoulder shrugs, slumped posture.
- Screechy or loud voice, mumbled speech, interruptions.
- Poor grammar, incorrect vocabulary.
- Wrinkled or ill-fitting clothing.

Inappropriate clothing, too much jewelry.

Excessive makeup or unkept hair.

Unpolished shoes.

Weak handshake or other non-verbal gestures.

Overlooked introductions.

Poor dining habits.

And the list could go on.

We have always heard you never get a second chance to make a first impression. In sixty-seconds or less, you have labeled yourself to someone you have just met or to someone who has observed your behavior.

As stated elsewhere in this book, manners follow you wherever you go. They will follow you as you enter a room, seat yourself before someone interviewing you for a job, meet the person you are asking for a charitable donation, join a guest at the dining table, as you are introduced to your future mother-in-law, or sit before your instructor (or stand before your students) for your first class meeting. We have the power to control the impression we make. To move toward a positive first impression:

Use a full-length mirror to check appearance before leaving home.

Record your voice—and listen to it.

Study communication practices—verbal and non-verbal—again, check the mirror.

Clean and press your clothing.

Have a makeup demonstration.

Make a professional barber/salon appointment.

Buy shoe polish—and use it.

- Practice a firm handshake (depending on your culture).
- Practice good posture—while checking the mirror.
- Become familiar with proper introductions, eye contact (depending on your culture), and good dining manners (see chapters in this book).

Many of these topics can also be found on YouTube and are both entertaining and educational.

Brand yourself with positive statements: the behavior and appearance of a caring professional.

Most of you reading this chapter could no doubt honestly say you have given people, probably most everyone you meet, what I call the *30-second sweep* from head to toe. You have made your first impression of them. Of course, most of the people you meet probably do the same to you.

Is their first impression what you would want it to be?

Every item in the lists above is based on good manners. The way you present yourself to others speaks to how you want to be treated and how you treat yourself.

Jane Adams, a noted author, makes a comment in her book that it is difficult if not impossible to separate style and substance. Style being appearance; substance being ability.

This book was written as a follow-up to a radio talk show I hosted to call attention to positive communication and etiquette practices. When taken to heart, our behaviors will become habits of the professional YOU, who will stand out in a crowd as the model for both *style* and *substance*.

Dr. Janet T. Cherry, Author

Don't Forget Your Manners!
…With Quiz #1

1. The *magic* words, we grow up with from childhood are:
    a. Cookies and cream.
    b. Please and Thank You.

2. Where is the appropriate place for a name tag?
    a. On the left shoulder.
    b. On the right shoulder.

3. When visiting an executive's office for a job interview you should be seated:
    a. When invited to be seated and in the seating offered.
    b. Upon entering the office, seat yourself near the desk.

4. What communication skill is most likely to prevent the most errors?
    a. Writing.
    b. Listening.

5. Which seat is designated as the place of honor at a formal dinner?
    a. The seat to the right side of the host/hostess.
    b. The seat to the left side of the host/hostess.

(Answers on page 191)

?QUESTIONING?

"Judge a man by his questions
rather than by his answers."
--Voltaire

The author, Dorothy Leeds, points out in her book, *Smart Questions*, we, in this culture, tend to make more statements than we ask questions. Questions enhance conversation; smart questions allow a complete set of facts for consideration and decision.

Even Dr. Seuss mentions that questions are often more complicated than the answers, especially when there has been little to no thought given before asking a question.

You might ask, what do questions have to do with manners? Think for a moment about questions you have been asked. Were they demeaning? Were they an invasion of privacy? Were they offensive in voice tone or word selection? All of the above signal a lack of respect.

Have you ever been in a situation where you are asked to complete a form and while doing so you are bombarded with a series of questions? Another example of how questioning and the questioner can show a lack of manners--*respect*.

My guest was Toni Johnson who resides in the Hudson Valley area of New York. Toni and I met when we were members of the National Advisory Council for Chapters of the American Society for Training and Development. (ASTD) Toni's coaching centers on executive leadership, life, and organization development. She aligns people skills with business processes for maximum outcomes.

Below, Toni shares how she uses effective questioning as her foundation for client success.

Initially, client and coach must establish a comfortable rapport. This is accomplished by accepting a set of mutually agreeable "guidelines" for working together and building a confidential relationship. An assessment of client needs is based on effective questioning and the analysis of information shared to attain desired outcomes or goals. Through effective or "smart" questioning you will:

Establish respect and trust as your mutual spoken or unspoken rules of every exchange.

Select a setting to foster concentration and reflection.

Prepare for your meeting. Design your questions to ensure your fact-finding will be clear and straightforward. You want to create building blocks leading to decisions and action.

Use a variety of question types: open, closed, and probing. These are defined below:

Closed questions provide only a one-word answer or body motion such as a shrug. Questions beginning with "would," "should," "is," "are," and "do you think," all lead to "yes" or "no."

Open questions with
  "who,"
    "what,"
      "when,"
        "where,"
          "why," and
            "how"

lead to people giving some thought to their answer. This will, most times, provide additional information.

Probing questions start with one point from an open or closed question's answer. It's like peeling back the layers of an onion until you finally get to the core of needed information to move forward. Keep in mind the wisdom of toddlers asking—**why? why?** and **why?**

 **Never** overlook the need for silence. People need time to reflect. Respect that need. It is not necessary to fill the air with constant noise.

Observe body language. The eyes and body movement will signal when to speak again.

Remember where there is a conflict between the spoken and unspoken word, the nonverbal is accepted as truth almost without exception.

Keep in mind all questions need—and deserve— answers. These answers will direct the exchange to the next level.

Show compassion and patience. Be attentive to the feelings of satisfaction and/or frustration a person expresses through responding to questions.

Sharpen your questioning skills. Effective questioning is a major component of the total communication process. It should also be noted the best take-away—even with the very best of questioning techniques, will only be captured through quality and active listening.

Toni Johnson *is a master practitioner certified in Neurolinguistic Programming through Catalyst, Inc. and The Brief Therapy Institute in Miami, Florida. She is also a certified trainer of Tracom Producing Results with Others. Toni has over 25 years of making a difference through cultural, team, and individual skill assessment analyzes for client success through appropriate solution options.*

COMMUNICATING ASSERTIVELY AND RESPECTFULLY

"A leader is best when people barely know he exists, when his work is done, his aim fulfilled, they will say: we did it ourselves."

--Lao Tzu

What, exactly, is assertive communication? I asked this question some 20 years ago when reviewing a conference agenda. It piqued my interest and I attended. That was the beginning of a new communication style for me—a concept that blends beautifully with both etiquette and listening: my passions.

Definition: Assertive communication is the ability to express positive and negative ideas and feelings in an open, honest, and direct way. Assertive communication recognizes our rights while still respecting the rights of others.

My guest was Toni Johnson, whom I met when serving on the National Advisory Council for Chapters, (American Society for Training and Development--ASTD). Our friendship and professional exchange has continued. Below are key points from our conversation regarding the principles and learning behaviors of assertive communication and its benefits.

Assertive communication components

There are three key components: *tone of voice, body language, and choice of words*. To incorporate all three in congruence requires thought and practice. If you are

speaking with positive words yet your body language is expressed negatively, the positive intent of your message is overcome by your negative behavior.

The formula focuses on "I" statements. Traditionally, we focus on "You" statements.

The receiver of an assertive communication request acknowledges in positive verbiage, follows with a response expressing feelings, and ends with a response stating what is wanted.

Tips for showing respect when speaking assertively

Keep tone of voice, body language, and choice of words congruent and positive.

Display erect posture: show you are in control of your thoughts and statements.

Make direct eye contact with the speaker: eye contact is also a show of respect, if appropriate for the culture.

Be comfortable in expressing your feelings and wants: positive or negative.

Listen attentively to what is being said: again, a show of respect.

Allow the receiver time to process the information and respond before interrupting with another message/question.

How are they showing respect?

Continue the exchange with open-ended questions to take the conversation to the next level. Probing questions allow you to peel back layers—like peeling an onion—and get to the real issues necessary to move the conversation forward.

Avoid misunderstandings and the communication "blame game" through assertive statements and responses.

What is happening here?

Below is an example of an assertive exchange. The example uses the three assertive statements. It is important to note that engaging in assertive communication initially may cause others to question your motives or interest. Most of us are creatures of habit and to change our pattern (or style) of communication, especially with someone you frequently engage in conversation, might seem confusing at first. Time and continued use usually bring understanding and appreciation for comfort, openness, and respect.

🎯 Example

You have been asked to be a speaker for a group meeting. You have spoken to this group on several occasions.

I realize you need a speaker for your dinner next month. However, I feel you need to introduce a different speaker to your group.
Therefore, I want to be your guest speaker at your April meeting—in four months.

The introductory words (however and therefore) are used for comfort in learning this communication style. When you become polished in speaking assertively, eliminate them. Their use is a good way to continue your complete statement without interruption.

In the above example, you have:

<u>Acknowledged</u> the request for a speaker;
  <u>Stated</u> your true feelings; and
    <u>Stated</u> what you want to do about the request and why.

You have offered your services which shows you are not dismissing neither the need nor the request.

Along with your statement, your body language will be pleasant, your tone of voice pleasant, and your words positive by offering yourself at another time.

I encourage you to give it a try.

PRACTICE IT—
PRACTICE IT AGAIN—
USE IT!

Everything is hard before it is easy.
- Goethe

Toni Johnson *resides in the Hudson Valley area of New York. She is a master practitioner certified in Neurolinguistic Programming through Catalyst, Inc. and The Brief Therapy Institute in Miami, Florida. She is also a certified trainer of Tracom Producing Results with Others. Toni has over 25 years of making a difference through cultural, team, and individual skill assessment analyzes for client success through appropriate solution options.*

MANNERS IN CONVERSATION

"The art of conversation is the art of speaking as well as being heard."
--William Hazlett

True conversation requires much more than meets the eye when two or more people are engaged in a verbal exchange. The precise definition of conversation: the informal exchange of ideas by the spoken word.

Meaningful conversation engages the mind, body, voice, ears, and eyes. Certain conversations may have a purpose of social entertainment while others may be focused on problem solving or competitive business exchange. In either case, *respect* is essential.

My guest, Ali Agha, heads Think-Cycle, a consulting organization assisting firms in finding direction and solutions through the process of *thinking, listening, and questioning.* Ali reminds us below of the behaviors and opportunities to display "good manners" when engaged in conversation.

Thinking requires directed concentration; listening requires a trained ear; and, questioning requires a measure of curiosity. Each of the elements in this cycle: thinking, listening, and questioning must be based on respect for each individual in a conversation group.

I found the book, *Why Smart People Do Dumb Things: Lessons from the New Science of Behavioral Economics,* by Mortimer Feinberg and John Tarrant an interesting read.

The book follows the results of verbal exchanges in boardrooms. Consider how these behaviors and opportunities display "*good manners*" when engaged in conversation.

❶ Be mindful of the individuals involved. Each person has unique perceptions of what is heard and how it is framed. Don't discredit another's contribution with disruptive body language, apparent listening disconnects, or disinterest in questions injected into the conversation.

❷ Be courteous. Inappropriate eye and facial expressions draw attention and may create discomfort among speakers.

❷ Be open to accepting individual interpretation.

❸ Be comfortable in asking for confirmation of understanding.

❸ Be thoughtful in forming questions to further, rather than stall, creative thinking.

❷ Be open to listening—as opposed to "daydreaming"—while another person is speaking. Keep in mind listening is a learned skill.

❷ Be open to sharing insights and possible outcomes as they might apply to fulfilling future needs and offering competitive solutions.

❸ Be patient. Suspend judgment until questions are fully answered.

② It is important that we *listen* between the words just as we *read* between the lines. It is also important to

understand the value and power of knowing when to stay quiet. There is no communication "rule" that says silence should be avoided during the conversation. Silence gives us a time to digest what we are hearing and time to think of how what we are hearing might apply to specific situations.

There are also annoying conversation habits pulled from my files—no name for credit—to be careful to avoid:

Listens inattentively.

Dominates the conversation.

Fidgets and distracts with body language. The body never lies!

Has an unpleasant voice that's hard to listen to.

Talks about **ME**, not **WE**.

Checks mobile devices all throughout the conversation.

Doesn't go beyond the weather for topics.

Argues and insists on being right.

Has a limited vocabulary which is repeated again and again.

 Gossips negatively about friends, co-workers, and others.

It is often revealing to ask yourself—or better yet, ask someone you can rely on for feedback if you are guilty of any of these behaviors.

Ludwig Wittgenstein, an Austrian philosopher, reminds us

"The limits of language mean the limits of our world."

Lastly, conversations are powered by responsible interaction.

Ali Agha, *a chemical engineer by training, works with organizations on developing leaders and managing risk to enhance resilience and value.*

KINDNESS

*"No act of kindness, no matter how small,
is ever wasted."*

--Aesop

In preparing for this show I reflected on my own impressions of kindness. It came to me that I view "kindness" as our personal, internal "manners" system. Manners, you can learn. Kindness is built-in. Manners come with rules: what, when, where, and how. Kindness is creative and more spontaneous.

There are websites offering suggestions for acts of kindness. It occurs to me that situation, time, and the individuals involved will find a "right thing to do." Just in case you need a starter or nudge, visit
*http://www.oprah.com/spirit/35-Little
Acts-of-Kindness#ixzz3iXjA7MoL*
for 35 ideas.

For teachers and trainers, visit *lifevestinside.com* for a kindness curriculum. Here is a sample of a kindness card or a "caught in the act" manners card that we have developed.

My "kindness" guest was Mike Sondag, a kind person. I met Mike when I led a session for a professional association. He was a director. Later, I facilitated workshops for his employees. Our conversation focused on the positive and personal benefits of providing happy moments and memories through simple—and often free—acts of kindness. We agreed that it is also nice to be the receiver.

Below are Mike's thoughts about kindness.

Giving someone a happy moment never goes out of style. Actually, there is a built-in reward in every gift because your act will also make you feel happy. It's a win-win.

Remember the statement almost everyone has heard: it takes more muscles to frown than to smile. So, why don't we see more smiles? One small, kind gesture can change a person's day. It may even be a reminder to pass it forward.

What is holding us back?

I like to send cards and always tuck a personal note inside.

While there are plenty of special occasions where cards are appropriate (Birthday, Holidays, Get Well, Sympathy, and Anniversary among others) the simple "Thinking of You" card is my favorite. The caption says it all. Keep a directory, selection of cards, stamps, and a calendar on hand to make this quick and easy.

Another quick way to say "I am thinking of you" is to clip and send articles from a newspaper or magazine—even a cartoon—or, in this age, just forward or attach to an email, again with a personal note. Neither cards nor clippings carry a large investment either in cost or time.

The internet posting mentioned above and several others I visited listed simple—many free—ideas for random acts of kindness to pass forward. I am passing on to you those I especially liked.

☺ **Give** a smile to those you meet: on the street, in the garage, at the office, in the store, in the park--everywhere.

☺ **Express** your gratitude to someone who has made a difference in your life.

☺ **Praise** someone at work for a job well done—from the highest to the lowest rank of employee, all like a pat on the back and extra words of kindness.

☺ **Listen** to people with interest, compassion, and concern. (Note: Listening turned up on all five of the lists I searched. It is also a great way to display good manners.)

☺ **Let** someone into traffic when there is a jam.

☺ **Offer** the person behind you in a checkout line who has only one or two items to go ahead of you. (This is Janet's favorite!)

☺ **Shop** for someone who is homebound or ill.

☺ **Share** flowers from your garden with a neighbor or friend.

☺ **Pass** on your magazines or papers to others.

☺ **Express** your appreciation for exceptional service at a restaurant to the server's manager before you leave.

☺ **Give** a presentation to a classroom of students on your area of expertise or on a subject you are passionate about.

☺ **Read** a book to a child or an elderly person.

☺ **Donate** a piece of clothing for every piece you buy.

👑 **Adopt** a pet. This pet may become your best friend!

👑 **Give** hugs generously when and where they are needed.

👑 **Say** "please" and "thank you"—often and sincerely. And, say "I'm sorry" and "excuse me" just as often and sincerely.

👑 **Treat** everyone with respect. **Period. No exceptions**.

👑 **Give** recognition to someone for a job well done on social media or in a public meeting.

👑 *Show kindness to yourself!*

These are just a few thoughts we mentioned in our conversation for moving kindness forward. According to a poll conducted by *Kindness USA*, (2016) only 25 percent of Americans believe we're living in a kind society. We can do better than that! We must have and show **R-E-S-P-E-C-T** to ourselves and others.

"One kind act is better than a thousand kind thoughts."

  --Unknown

Michael R. Sondag *is a retired executive having worked with international corporations, national franchises, and professional associations throughout a 40-year career. Recognized for growth and achievement through professional development and creative marketing, he is also a believer in demonstrating respect and good manners for all people.*

LISTENING

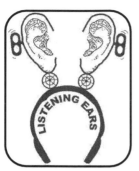

*"I know you believe you understand
what you think I said,
but I am not sure you realize
that what you heard is not what I meant."*
--Author Unknown

Listen up now...are you listening?
These words have probably been heard
in most classrooms. Admittedly, I am guilty. I have also
asked this of family, meeting attendees, and workshop
participants. Not to offer an excuse this might have
happened because I had not studied listening as a skill.

In the mid 90's I was attracted to an invitation announcing a
conference sponsored by The International Listening
Association (ILA). The material peaked my interest and I
attended. My husband's chiding prompted me to invite him.
He found humor in my wanting to attend a conference on
listening and quite funny that I should invite him!

Well, I learned how to listen; he didn't.
Years forward this proved a valuable
skill at home and professionally. (I
learned that I could get what I wanted if
I asked when he was not listening which was most of the
time—a beautiful thing!)

I joined ILA and became the Association president in 1999.
My passion for listening has only increased especially when
I ventured into becoming certified as an etiquette coach. *To
have someone truly listen to you is the hallmark of respect!*
Visit the ILA website (*www.ILA.org*) for exceptional
resources on listening.

My guest for this program was Clare Novak of Chester Springs, Pennsylvania. Clare is a friend and colleague. We met as co-members of the National Advisors to Chapters, American Society for Training and Development (ASTD). Clare heads Novak and Associates and is an international Human Resources and Leadership Development Consultant. I was happy to have Clare join me to get her perspective on Listening from both a national and international focus. Below are her thoughts.

From Hearing to Listening

The first statement I want to make pertains to Janet's experience with her husband. Many people share his view on why go to learn how to listen? The answer is, *we are not born knowing how to listen. Hopefully, we are born knowing how to hear!*

This gift has to be developed and transformed from a **"hearing" ear into a *"listening" ear** as well.* Listening is the process of receiving, constructing meaning from, and responding to spoken and/or nonverbal messages. (The International Listening Association.)

Why Listen?

Listening is critical. Listening is learned. Listening is a communication skill affecting you, the person, and you, the professional. Effective listening skills also impact your happiness and fulfillment as well as your company's bottom line. *Listening shows respect to the speaker.*

As a Strength Coach, I am very aware of the need to strengthen those skills you have and to build those skills you need to develop. In my professional role and using Strength Finder Assessments' feedback, I focus on my clients' mind, heart, natural talents, and abilities as gifts you bring to this world. These gifts may not be strengths until time and energy are invested to enable more productivity. I enjoy the process used with my clients because it comes out of positive psychology—what is right with you; what you can do with your positive strengths to have more energy to contribute to a more satisfying result. While what you do best is reinforced; weaknesses are managed.

Communication is our foundation. Listening is a big part. Research (ILA 2001 – Wolf and Coakley) stated daily use of our recognized communication skills breaks down as:

writing	9%
reading	15%
speaking	30%
listening	45-55%

These are the latest figures available. Keep in mind, technology advancements and increased cell phone usage may give us different figures today. The point here suggests listening is a major component of our daily lives. Unfortunately, there is evidence that in many educational institutions there is not respective time devoted to learning to listen.

Are Listening Habits Universal?

My clients are located worldwide. This has allowed me to become more aware of differences in communication practices. Head nodding as a listener, for example, is not the same in all cultures. In our culture, a vertical nod means "yes." A vertical nod in other cultures may not mean "yes" but "agreement with what you are saying, or maybe." And a "maybe" might mean "no." A horizontal nod by a listener in our culture means "no." Whereas, in other cultures, it may not always mean "no."

ⓠ Preparation

Before traveling to any unfamiliar location, national or international, prepare yourself for the cultural differences. This includes spoken, written, and listening.

- Read about the customs of communication.
- Learn nonverbal practices and their meanings.
- Know the differences in styles of listening and how to "read" their meaning.
- Be prepared to spend time over casual meetings and many cups of tea, coffee, or the preferred beverage getting to know the person(s) who will be involved in your conversations and negotiations.
- Allow yourself to become comfortable with your message and how to respond. Here again, listening skills are critical.
- Learn the four elements involved in effective listening:

Hear the message: pay attention, select what is important, and recognize emotional messages.

Interpret the message: use self-knowledge, a desire to understand, and ask questions for clarification.

Evaluate the message: ask probing questions if necessary, analyze the evidence, and don't jump to conclusions.

Respond to the message: acknowledge the message was

heard, and there is a desire to reach a common understanding. Give feedback, attempt to avoid confusing responses, and move to final agreement of evaluation and proposed action.

Listening Distractions

There are six common listening styles, each with its own characteristics. For speakers, consultants,

educators, and managers/business professionals it is an advantage to become familiar with at least the major characteristic of each style to stay "in tune" with responses. These are:

Leisure: Relaxed, needs to be interested to hear the spoken word; "day dreamer."

Inclusive: Knows everything; attentive to *all* words; needs exactness about the topic to hear it.

Stylistic: Who, How, What? Needs credentials—why should I listen to you?

Technical: Things, not people oriented; Wants the "how."

Empathetic: People, not things oriented; processes nonverbal; cares about feelings.

Non-conforming: Listens for mistakes; evaluates critically.

In keeping with these styles, there are also the cultural communication disrupters to consider: extreme hand movement; interrupting when others are speaking; or everyone talking at the same time, as examples. Effective listening is difficult under these circumstances. In our culture, *these distractors are all elements of rudeness and considered poor manners. They may also be considered "normal behaviors"—even good manners—in other cultures.*

In our daily lives we will interact with people all along the listening spectrum—from the "highly interested" intent on getting full information—to the "could care less" group who had rather not be involved. Knowing how to cope with a variety of communication situations is the challenge. In order to listen actively:

Choose to listen.

Listen for information and facts.

Listen to yourself.

Listen with the ♥'s *ear.*

Know when to keep quiet.

Good Listening IS Good Manners!

Clare Novak *is an award-winning international Human Resources and Leadership Development Consultant with over 25 years' experience. She is a sought-after speaker and noted author, having addressed multiple international conferences. Her international experience in utilities, telecom, and transportation includes Europe, Middle East Asia, and Africa as well as North America.*

WORKPLACE MANNERS AND INTERNAL COMMUNICATION

"Communication—the human connection—is the key to personal and career success."

--Paul J. Meyer

One of the practices in the Management Department at The University of Memphis was to invite guests from the business community to visit our classrooms. Participants in the program were assigned to a class. My guest was Liz McKee, Director of Internal Communications with Baker Donelson law firm. Her classroom detail was to conduct mock interviews, to have a conversation with our students about the importance of positive communications in the workplace, and—how to fit in as "the new kid on the block." The students enjoyed her visits. I also enjoyed them and was happy for the opportunity to welcome Liz for several semesters.

 This law firm is very prestigious both locally and nationally, being the 53rd largest in the nation. The firm is home to some 750+ attorneys and over 1500+ employees located in 24 offices throughout the South and in D.C. For eight consecutive years, the firm has been recognized and listed on Fortune's 100 Best Companies To Work For.

When I reviewed topics selected for the radio shows, Liz McKee immediately came to mind for workplace manners and internal communication. Liz graciously agreed to share a Saturday morning with me and our listeners. Our conversation focused on how her firm incorporates a busy environment with respect for clients and for each other.

Below are her comments on how to establish this same feeling of appreciation and respect within every office, large or small.

Don't think size—think mindset. We spend more time with our office family than we do with our personal family. Our firm believes the result we want to achieve begins in the hiring process. We work hard to ensure we attract and retain people who value and practice respect and kindness in the workplace.

Our CEO jokes, but it is true, we have a "no-jerk" hiring policy. Our work is hard enough. There is no room for disrespect—it makes the work that much more difficult. Key role: keeping 1500+ employees *connected* through factual and timely information. Communication is key in every situation and always better learned—good or bad—through organized, internal channels rather than from outside leaks. This communication outreach is based on the four core values embraced by our firm:

- *One Firm*. Emphasizes external clients and internal clients (our employees) working together.
- *Clients First*. We are all here to serve our client base and their needs—whatever it takes.
- *Shared Beliefs*. Integrity, Diversity, Accomplishment, Mutual Respect, and Support. These beliefs extend to clients, to people in the community, and to one another.
- *Smart Growth*. Growth is not for the sake of expanding numbers but as the need occurs to serve our clients better.

When employees feel valued and cared for, they, in turn, pass this care, concern, and respect on to our clients. Below are reminders for all employees to make the work environment more enjoyable and less stressful:

❖ *Be responsible*. Do what you say you will do and let your behavior patterns bear out your words of commitment:

- Deadlines, updates, attention to detail, cooperation—whatever it takes to meet the need.

❖ *Be aware of surroundings*. Cell phones fall into this category:

- Move to a private place for private conversations.
- Keep your voice down—the people around you should not lose concentration because of your call.

- Mute your phone while in meetings. The person in front of you should have primary attention.

❖ *Be mindful of office courtesies*.

- If the copy machine is out of paper when your job is finished, be sure to fill it up, and don't leave a jam.
- If you take the last note pad, alert the person who orders supplies.
- If you see a lunch in the office refrigerator and it looks good, just *wish* it were yours and close the door.
- If you have the last cup of coffee, make a fresh pot.
- If you are engaged at the elevator, don't hold the elevator to continue the conversation.
- If you make a mistake, admit it. Don't pass the buck.
- If you make a mess in the kitchen, bathroom, or at your desk, clean it up.

(We have 12 standards of excellence and one of them reads, "Our appearance, work spaces, and public areas reflect our commitment to excellence.")

Be conscious of your communication style and practice.

- Watch tone of voice and choice of words.
- Be aware of body language.
- Speak to others with a "hello," "please," "thank you," "you are welcome," and "enjoy your evening." Remember, the "magic words" are not just for children.
- Ask for clarification if you don't understand an instruction or statement.
- Remember cultural differences: eye contact, greetings, time, food, and even driving. Help with introducing these differences to co-workers when needed.
- Be patient—don't interrupt the person speaking.
- Be on time. Promptness is both communication and consideration.

Be mindful of meeting manners.

- If there are not sufficient items for an agenda or regularly held meetings, cancel and communicate information through email or text.
- Review the meeting agenda before the meeting.
- Be on time.
- Be a good listener.
- If unable to attend, let the meeting chair know.
- Bring reports or documents for which you are responsible.
- Keep cell phone on mute. If you are expecting a call, excuse yourself.
- Do not interrupt the chair or other speakers.
- Excuse yourself if you must leave before the chair adjourns the meeting.

❖ *Be open to connections, recognition, and appreciation. Make them feel a part of something. Integrate a new employee by:*

- Inviting them to lunch.
- Introducing them during daily team meeting.
- Sending a card thanking them for choosing our firm.
- Thanking employee's family for supporting the decision to join our firm.
- Recognizing birthday or employment anniversary.
- Showing appreciation for a project well done.

There are many ways an employer can show recognition and appreciation for the effort and consideration employees put forth both for clients and for co-workers. Be aware of the human needs of every individual and the energy and effort that boosts enthusiasm and loyalty. A handwritten "Thank You" takes only a few minutes. These little things mean a lot to all employees—new or tenured. They show respect— they show good manners. They show why a company is ranked among the BEST!

Elizabeth McKee has more than 17 years of experience in the communications field. A former news anchor, reporter, and producer, Liz has worked in the employee communications and engagement field for ten years. In addition to motivating employees through strategic communication, she also manages her firm's client service, community service, wellness, and environmental programs.

Don't Forget Your Manners!

…When Preparing for and Attending Meetings

🐾 Confirm your attendance or absence to a meeting notice to the Chair, Secretary, or person stated.

🐾 Come prepared. Review the Agenda and note items you wish to question or discuss.

🐾 Prepare reports which are your responsibility. If unable to attend, have someone give the report for you and distribute appropriate documents.

🐾 Arrive on time.

🐾 Introduce yourself to new attendees and make them feel welcome.

🐾 Turn off your cell phone.

🐾 Listen attentively. Don't talk while others are talking.

🐾 Raise your hand to be acknowledged by the Chair.

🐾 Ask for clarification if you are confused about something.

🐾 Separate issues from people and focus on issues. No cheap shots or insults.

🐾 Speak only for yourself. Always be respectful of others and their opinions. (You can disagree without being disagreeable.)

🐾 Do your part to keep the meeting focused on Agenda items.

🐾 Keep your seat until the meeting has been adjourned.

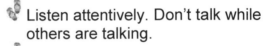

THE INTERVIEW

"Success will more likely knock on your door if you are prepared and self-confident."

--Marjorie Stute

There was a time in my career when I owned a résumé and interview service—over 30 years ago. I still remember one young man who told me he needed "words" and his friend had sent him to me.

I asked about the job he wanted. It was as a kitchen assistant in a restaurant near his home and he needed it desperately. "He could pay me after he got the job if that would be OK," he said. He knew he could do this job better than anyone who applied if he had the words. We didn't have much experience to go on as this was his first job but he had a winning attitude and self-confidence. We went to work and got his words on paper and prepared him to say them in an interview. I thought I might never hear from him again. A few weeks later he came back to my office. He was beaming and had a rose and an envelope in his hand. "Thank you," he said. "This is for you." The envelope held a $2 first payment.

Attitude and self-confidence were both a part of our conversation on interviewing. My guest was Agnes Pokrandt, a partner in Reach Human Capital, an employment consulting firm based in Memphis, Tennessee. Agnes and I have known each other professionally for many years and it was a treat to catch up with her and hear of her accomplishments. We had a great conversation. Interviews

67

are tricky and they require both traits of the young man I met many years ago: positive attitude and self-confidence. Here are Agnes' tips for job search preparation: the résumé and cover letter, the interview, and the follow-up.

Certainly, I agree. Interviews can be tricky. There are so many unknown factors—on both sides of the desk. *Preparation is key whether you are in a job search for your first job or desiring an upward move.*

Keep in mind you show good manners and respect for the interviewing company and its representatives in every stage of the process by presenting documents that are neat, clean, in good business taste, complete, and written in clear statements. Also, in good taste and following good manners is presenting yourself professionally.

Interview Preparation Step One: The Résumé

- 👍 Have a copy of the position announcement in front of you when you develop your résumé.

- 👍 Search the internet for résumé templates to find one you like that is appropriate. Follow it.

- 👍 Write your résumé in your personal style of self-expression yet always with good grammar and spelling. Résumés are written in third person.

- 👍 Remember to include transferable skills and attributes: customer service, organization, time management, and dependability (all needed in every business) as they will apply in a new situation.

- 👍 Include your accomplishments and how they had impact on the company's bottom line.

👍 Leave white space rather than wall-to-wall words. Use no smaller than a 12-pitch font, "résumé" paper, and black ink.

👍 Be sure to have contact information: phone, email, and mail. (a professional email address—not "hot mama" or such.)

👍 Send a copy to yourself to check the format when printed.

Interview Preparation Step Two: The Cover Letter

👍 Search the internet for cover letter templates.

👍 Use paper matching your résumé for the cover letter—and again black ink.

👍 Follow the information provided in the position announcement to address the letter. Use a title.

👍 State the position you are referencing and how you heard about it in the first paragraph.

👍 Keep in mind your cover letter is a sales tool to focus on skills and accomplishments listed in your résumé and how they match the position's requirements.

👍 Be sure your full contact information is either on your letterhead or following your signature.

👍 Be sure you sign your letter—again in black ink.

Interview Preparation Step Three: The Interview

👍 Research the company extending the position announcement. The internet will provide information on products, service, establishment, growth, and mission. Review the annual report which will give financial data.

👍 Have a conversation with an employee, if you know one.

👍 Read local publications which might state company awards, outstanding accomplishments, community involvement.

👍 Read both positive and negative reviews—mention only the positive ones.

Interviewing practices have changed over the years and today most first interviews are conducted in a telephone conversation. These "first interviews" are generally to weed out applicants. Just a few tips if your first interview is a scheduled phone call.

👍 Keep by your phone: a copy of the position announcement, a copy of your résumé, a pen and pad, and a list of questions 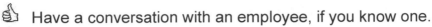 you have from reading the position description.

👍 Stand in good posture while you are talking with the company representative. This allows your oxygen to move freely through your body, giving you an energetic sound and feeling.

👍 Use good listening practices. This includes not interrupting the speaker and respecting all comments. (You might want to review the section in this book on Listening.)

👍 Make it a point to ask what's next in their interviewing process. Also, ask if a time frame is known for the next step.

👍 Be sure to thank the person calling for reading your résumé package and for the call itself.

If you have made it through the résumé review and the first phone interview and if you are invited for a personal interview, here are more tips. This time, you are not hiding behind a phone.

👍 Research the location where the interview will take place.

👍 Get a good night's rest. Eat a healthy meal.

👍 Prepare your portfolio with a copy of your résumé, a pad and pen, your questions, business card, and Kleenex.

👍 Leave in plenty of time to be a few minutes early for your appointment.

👍 Get yourself and your clothes in good order:

- Ladies wear dress or suit; gentlemen a jacket, shirt, trousers, and tie. No T-shirts.
- Wear shoes (closed toe) AND socks/hose. No flip flops. No tennis shoes. Shoes should be polished.
  - Clothes should fit well and be fresh, clean, and pressed.
  - Hair should be clean and neatly combed.
  - Fingernails should be clipped and clean.
- Take time for a final look in the mirror before heading out.

👍 Park in the appropriate place.

👍 Have a warm smile for everyone you meet.

👍 Greet the person who will interview you with a firm handshake.

👍 Wait to be seated until invited.

👍 Don't play with your hair, clothing, or your portfolio.

👍 ***Leave your cell phone in the car.***

👍 Have limited jewelry—one ring for each hand, and one pair of earrings.

👍 LISTEN carefully to what the interviewer is saying.

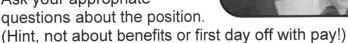

👍 Wait to answer until he/she has finished speaking.

👍 Ask your appropriate questions about the position. (Hint, not about benefits or first day off with pay!)

👍 Be sure you know what the next step in the hiring process will be before you leave.

👍 Ask for a business card before leaving.

👍 When the interview is over, thank the person, shake hands, and exit professionally.

Interview Preparation Step Four: The Follow-Up

👍 Write your follow-up letter within 24-48 hours. *Note*: A follow-up letter should be written after each interview, and as well if you are rejected for this position.

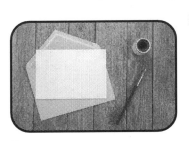

👍 Use this letter as an additional way to market yourself. Information from the interview will give you the content by showing how you are a match for the position.

👍 Be sure you address the letter and the envelope with a title (Mr., Mrs., Ms., Doctor, Judge, etc.).

👍 Remember to sign the letter.

👍 Be prepared for a drug test, credit check, and questions regarding social media IF you are offered the position.

Interview Preparation Final Thoughts

👍 It is becoming more common for final interviews to be conducted over a meal. This could be breakfast, lunch, or dinner. For younger people, lunch is the most common option. For older people and management or executive positions, dinner is usually the choice.

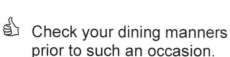

👍 Check your dining manners prior to such an occasion. (You might want to refer to the sections in this book for information on dining manners.)

Our conversation could have lasted for much longer; however, our show was just one hour. This is a start. Read it. Review it. Use it. The information here will be a great place to begin your job search preparation.

"Sometimes it takes 100 'no's' before you get one 'yes'."
--A. McNeill

Agnes M. Pokrandt, *after success in corporate business, created AMP Associates and later co-founded REACH Human Capital, focusing on individuals who had been downsized and in job search. Presently, her focus is tutoring international business professionals, transferred by a Memphis company, in English as a second language.*

Don't Forget Your Manners!
...In the Hospital or Visiting
    the Sick

Take a bow for thinking about friends who are ill or recovering from an illness. Think twice about how best to comfort them.

Make a call to the home, hospital, or rehab center before showing up. Confirm visitors are allowed and the hours of visitation.

Ask about flowers before sending or bringing them.

Make visits short. Patients are often "busy" with lab, exercise, or other scheduled activities.

Ask what you can do to assist the patient or the family— handle mail, check on a pet, run an errand, deliver a message, or find a favorite book or magazine.

Resist bringing "goodies" until you have checked.

Remember both children and pets can be comforting if they are mannerly and if they are allowed as visitors.

Show respect for the patient by stepping out of the room when medical personnel arrive.

Keep telephone conversations short.

Get Well Soon!

Express your thoughts and wishes with a card and a special note inside if calls or visitors are not allowed.

Remember, speaking is often as comforting as presence.

DRESS FOR SUCCESS

"Your mirror can be your best--or worst--friend."
--Clemmy Lee Benson

Today's program was especially enjoyable to me. I am always excited when I am invited to speak to a group preparing for an initial interview or seeking that next opportunity. Someone else has prepared them for the specific skills required. Has anyone had a conversation with them regarding their appearance, manners, or body language, and their importance in landing that position? Sometimes not.

For women, there is an international program, Dress for Success, founded in 1997, whose purpose is to offer assistance—and the clothing—to create a professional image. Whether we realize it or not, our appearance empowers us to achieve our full potential—put our best foot forward, build self-esteem, and display confidence.

To our women readers who may be looking for a volunteer opportunity, I suggest checking out the Dress for Success Foundation—*http://www.dressforsuccess.org*. There is a local chapter in Memphis, Tennessee, and in 145 other cities in 23 countries. It's a great feeling to know you have made a difference in helping someone move ahead to achieve personal potential.

My guest for today's conversation, Evonne Siemer, does just that. I met Evonne when I joined our Gavel Club, an organization whose members have all served as presidents of civic and/or professional groups. I quickly learned Evonne and I had a mutual respect for helping to initiate or restore the practice of "good manners" including the importance of appearance and positive first impressions. Evonne conducts workshops based on the "dress for success" philosophy. Below are the highlights of our conversation.

When conducting *Dress for Success* workshops, it is important for participants to understand that success depends on the successful blending of skill, attitude, *and* appearance. Here are my key reminders and tips:

- Have a good mirror--*use it and believe it*. In fact, it's a good idea to have more than one: a full view and a smaller magnifier.

    Make a habit of a "last glance" before leaving home. Arrive for an appointment a few minutes early to visit the restroom for a final mirror check before your appointment.

    Shopping for clothes is another opportunity to trust the mirror. It is surprising how an expensive outfit can look so cheap! Likewise, with savvy shopping, the result can be a winner. Fit over fashion and label over fad is always a good decision. Present a coordinated and organized appearance and that is how you will be perceived.

- Remind yourself that looking good and feeling good enhance your image. A pleasant facial expression and a smile go a long way toward achieving success. Ladies, don't cover your natural, radiant glow with thick make-up applications. Use cosmetics moderately.

- Practice positive and complimentary body language. Non-verbal communication is more often believed over verbal statements. Be cautious about posture, how you are seated, how you walk, your gesturing, and how you move your body.

🔹 Smell fresh versus overpowering. You do not want to announce yourself through the selection of strong fragrances or an underuse of soap.

🔹 Dress appropriately for your role. Follow the company handbook. Neatness and cleanliness are expected in all levels of dress. If your employer embraces "casual Friday" or "dress-down day," be sure it is well defined and understood. In all instances, leave the flip flops, jogging suits or logo T-shirts for after work.

🔹 Select jewelry that is seen rather than heard. The jingle of jewelry is distracting to a conversation. Simple selections promote a coordinated and professional image.

🔹 Keep fingernails clean and trimmed. When you shake a person's hand, you neither want to scrape nor stab.

🔹 Cover your feet and polish your shoes. Your total dress for success appearance extends from head to toe.

You are creating your brand. Be consistent, be comfortable, be identified by your total presence: dress, positive attitude, and professional attention to responsibility.

These guidelines are just as important once you are in your professional setting as when you are interviewing. Your brand, once established, follows you through your career. Set the highest standards for yourself and keep them polished.

"People can't focus on your brain
if all eyes are on your dress."
--Anonymous

Evonne T. Siemer *is a native Tennessean. Her career includes serving as Director of Development for Brooks Museum of Art in Memphis, Tennessee. She is active in community organizations and as an events planner facilitates traditional teas and etiquette programs for children and adults.*

Don't Forget Your Manners!
…With Four Steps to a
Proper Handshake

- As you approach someone, extend your right arm when you are about three feet away. Slightly angle your arm across your chest, with your thumb pointing up.

- Lock hands, thumb joint to thumb joint. Then, firmly clasp the other person's hand, without any bone crushing or macho posturing.

- Pump the other person's hand two to three times.

- Let go.

A good handshake is important. It should be firm and held no more than three-to-four seconds. In our culture, eye contact accompanies the handshake. Ladies, it is acceptable for you to make the first move toward a handshake.

Lastly, if you are acting appropriately in initiating a handshake and the person to whom you have extended your hand does not reciprocate, say nothing, and simply move your hand back. There may be cultural differences.

An informal way to greet someone you know is a "high five" where right arms are raised, and the two people slap palms.

Another alternative is the "fist bump." Two people form right hands into a fist and gently bump one another's fist. Some people choose this because of not wanting to pass germs. On September 22, 2009, the Dalai Lama was welcomed to Memphis, Tennessee, not with a handshake but with a fist bump from interim Memphis Mayor Myron Lowery. The exiled Tibetan spiritual leader balled up his fist and reached it forward to make friendly contact with the mayor's own balled-up fist.

Don't Forget Your Manners!
...Formal Dining Faux Pas

Back: Left to Right
Hostess in long dress:
Removing food before guest finished
Serving dessert before everyone finished
Female Guest with curls:
Inappropriate outfit
Straw in wine glass
Didn't use napkin
Female Guest with long hair:
Putting on lipstick at table
Iced beverage spoon in glass
Didn't use napkin
Male Guest standing:
Standing before everyone finished
Stacked up plates/utensils
Male Guest sitting:
Napkin in shirt
Pushing plate away
Water glass on wrong side
Licking lips
Female Guest with pony tail:
Cell phone
Knife on wrong side of plate
Arms resting on food
Female Guest with heels:
Resting feet on empty chair
3 glasses of wine
Napkin wadded on table
Plates stacked up

Front: Right to Left
Male Guest with beard
Cut up all meat at once
Bread on salad plate
Passing pepper, not salt as well
Knife resting in wrong place
Grabbing wine glass
Bread plate in wrong place
Female Guest sitting
Pointing with fork
5 rolls
Male Guest sitting
Buttering all of roll
Wine glass in wrong place
Napkin on floor
Female Guest sitting
Smoking at table
Dessert fork and spoon on salad plate
If finished, knife and fork in wrong place
Butter knife not on plate
Roll on dinner plate
Legs crossed, not under table
Male Guest sitting
Gripping fork
Knife stuck in roll

Seating should be male, female, male, female, etc.

FORMAL DINING TABLE SETTING

"Don't let your appetite spoil your manners."
--Henry Moon

Dining experiences vary from casual to formal and many individual styles in between. Our busy lives indulge fast food, deli take-out, and grab-a-cracker-and-run. There is even a special category for eating at home: "single dining style." In a simple, five-question, unscientific survey of a dozen of my friends, I realized that most single dwellers have a pattern of *not* dining alone even when they *are* alone. The questions and responses:

- Do you dine at a table? No, not always.
- Do you use matching place settings? No, not always.
- Do you use napkins? Yes, usually or paper towels.
- Do you use proper dining manners? Yes, always, just a bit modified since there is no one to pass food to nor wait to be seated so eating may begin.

There is always an awareness of dining etiquette: closed mouth when chewing, breaking bread and buttering one piece at a time, and using the appropriate utensils just to name a few.

We (yes, I am included) do not want to dine alone. We listen to music, the news, the weather, we watch the birds and other animals, a favorite program, or attend an on-line workshop. We eat on the patio, in front of TV, or at the computer! Does this sound strange? Not really when you think about it.

Consider the number of times you go to most any restaurant and see two people dining at a single table and no one is talking—they are both busy on cell phones! Where would you rather dine?

There are occasions when dining alone is not the ticket. We quickly admitted this truth. This is where the fifth question, the "big question" dropped.

- Can you still set a formal table properly when needed? The answer--a unanimous "yes, perfectly."

We also enjoy displaying proper social graces, sharing good conversation, and appreciating a beautifully appointed formal table.

Finally, we agreed. When you have learned the ritual of proper table appointments, then you have also earned the privilege of enjoying "single dining style" at its best. One entire radio broadcast was devoted to going through an explanation of each of the utensils—their placement and their purpose. This is shared below for our readers.

Use the diagrams in this chapter and the explanation of each item shown along with its position on the table for a more formal presentation.

The Napkin

The first item of business after being seated at the table is the napkin. Napkins usually coordinate with the tablecloth. If there is a napkin ring (which in today's world is purely for decoration) remove it and place it above the forks. They are neither a toy, nor a souvenir.

When the host/hostess and guests are seated, remove the napkin from the table and place it in your lap with a fold toward your body.

The napkin remains on your lap and ready for use to gently blot your mouth throughout the entire meal. The exception being if you need to leave the table before the end of the meal. In this event, place your napkin on the seat of your chair to alert the staff that you will return. Never use your napkin to signal your server, wipe your cutlery, or blow your nose. Never tuck the napkin into your shirt like a bib or into your pants/skirt.

When you have finished your meal, loosely refold your napkin and place it on the table to the left of your dinner plate. This lets the server know you are finished with your meal.

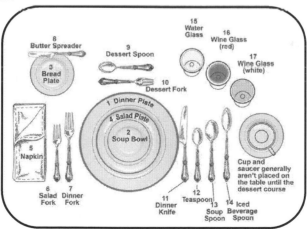

Silverware will be used from the outside in. To the left, salad fork before dinner fork. To the right, again from outside in, iced beverage spoon, soup spoon, teaspoon, and dinner knife with blade toward the plate. As an aside, once you have observed the pieces of silverware at your table setting, you can almost tell the courses you will be having for the meal. Looking at the picture in this chapter, you will be served soup, salad, an entrée, bread/rolls, an iced beverage, and a dessert. The coffee cup, saucer, and spoon are generally served with dessert.

1. *Dinner plate.* The center of the place setting. When finished eating, do not push the plate away from you. Instead, place both your fork and knife across the center of the plate, representing a clock time of 10:20 with 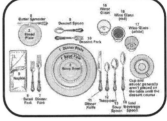 handles to the right, the knife blade facing you and the fork tines up. *Note:* Usually the dinner plate is not presented until the entrée is served.

2. *Soup bowl.* Usually served on a saucer. If you need to set your soup spoon down while eating, place it in the bowl. When you have finished, place it on the saucer or leave it in the bowl.

3. *Bread plate.* Positioned just above the forks. Bread should be broken into bite-sized pieces, not cut. Butter only one piece at a time—the piece you are planning to eat. Butter may be on your bread plate or it may be served.

4. **Salad plate.** Positioned in same place as dinner plate.

5. *Napkin.* The napkin was explained earlier.

6. *Salad fork.* The salad fork is placed to the left of the dinner fork.

7. *Dinner fork.* The dinner fork is placed to the left of the dinner plate. Usually, you will have no more than three forks: salad, fish, and dinner. There is no fish fork in this picture. The use is from outside in.

8. ***Butter spreader.*** The butter spreader is placed horizontally across the top of the bread plate.

9. ***Dessert spoon.*** The dessert spoon is placed above the plate with the handle facing right.

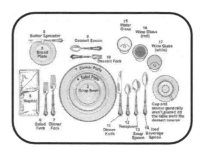

10. ***Dessert fork.*** The dessert fork is placed above the plate and below the dessert spoon with the handle facing left.

11. ***Dinner knife.*** The dinner knife is placed to the right of the dinner plate with the blade facing the plate. There may be meat, fish, and salad knives. There are no fish or salad knives in this picture. The order of use is from outside in.

12. ***Teaspoon.*** The teaspoon is placed to the right of the dinner knife.

13. ***Soup spoon.*** The soup spoon is placed to the right of the teaspoon. You will recognize the soup spoon by its rounded bowl.

14. **Iced beverage spoon.** If there is an iced beverage spoon, it would be placed to the right of the soup spoon.

15. ***Water glass.*** The water glass sits in line with the tip of the knife.

16. ***Red wine glass.*** The red wine glass sits slightly below and to the right of the water glass.

17. ***White wine glass.*** The white wine glass sits slightly below and to the right of the red wine glass.

Note: The coffee cup, saucer and spoon are often served after the entrée and with dessert.

Dining Etiquette Reminders

- Reply to invitations by the date requested.
- Place napkin in lap: use only to pat mouth.
- Keep elbows off the table during the meal.
- Remove spoon from cup/glass before drinking.
- Chew with mouth closed; don't overload mouth.
- Taste food before adding salt/pepper.
- Break bread. Butter one piece at a time.
- Cut meat one or two bites at a time.
- Place utensils at the 10:20 clock position when done.
- Place napkin, loosely folded, to left of plate when done.
- Thank host/hostess before leaving.

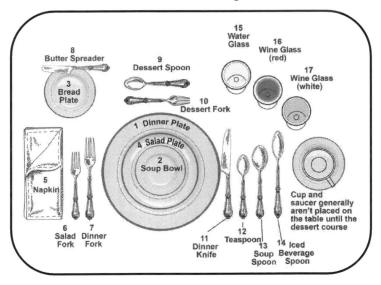

Note: This picture represents a place setting
for American-style dining.

Remember,
Manners Always Matter

Dr. Janet T. Cherry, Author

Don't Forget Your Manners!
... With Quiz #2

1. Forks are on which side of the dinner plate?
    a. Forks are on the right side of the dinner plate.
    b. Forks are on the left side of the dinner plate.

2. What is the purpose of the two utensils when placed at the top of your plate?
    a. The two utensils are used for salad and soup.
    b. The two utensils are used for dessert.

3. If your dinner partner asks for the pepper, you should
    a. Pass the pepper as requested.
    b. Pass the salt *and* pepper.

4. It is correct to cut your rolls rather than breaking them.
    a. No, you always break the rolls.
    b. Yes, cutting your rolls is correct.

5. After stirring your iced beverage, you should
    a. Leave the spoon in the glass to stir again later.
    b. Remove the spoon from the glass. Do not place it on the tablecloth.

(Answers on Page 191)

Don't Forget Your Manners!
...The Flag of The United States of America

🐾 Observe Flag Day in the United States on June 14.

🐾 Stand at attention during the Pledge of Allegiance.

🐾 Never allow the flag to be used for any advertising purpose. Neither should it be used as a part of a costume or athletic uniform.

🐾 Never should the flag have placed on it or attached to it, any mark, insignia, letter, word, number, figure, or drawing of any kind.

🐾 Display the flag only on days when the weather is not inclement. Illuminate the flag if it is displayed at night.

🐾 Hoist the flag briskly and lower it ceremoniously.

🐾 Display the flag so that it never touches anything beneath it, such as the ground, the floor, water, or merchandise. When lowered, it should be received by waiting hands and arms.

🐾 Clean and mend the flag when necessary. When it is so worn it is no longer fit to serve as a symbol of our country, it should be destroyed by burning in a dignified manner. Many post offices and veteran organizations have drop-off places, and they will destroy the flag in a ceremony.

🐾 Store the flag by folding it neatly.

🐾 *Give our flag, the Flag of the United States of America, the dignity it deserves and represents. Standing for the National Anthem is a show of respect.*

WINE AND ROSES

"Give me a bowl of wine—
in this I bury all
unkindness"

--Brutus
(William Shakespeare's Julius Caesar)

This show aired on Saturday, February 14, Valentine's Day. It is common knowledge to everyone who knows me; I confess to being a romantic. Valentine's Day is a personal favorite.

A beautiful love story of its own is how the celebration of Valentine's day began in the third century. What better way

to remember your special love and dear friends than with the sharing and celebration of chocolates, wine, fruit, and roses. (Of course, your personal flower of choice is also a great selection.)

Another of my SCORE volunteer buddies, Victor Robilio, graciously agreed to be my guest. He is a living fountain of wine knowledge. Victor shared many tips for following etiquette and displaying manners when selecting, serving, pouring, toasting, drinking, and enjoying wine.

From our conversation and listed below are selected tips for being a gracious host, hostess, or guest when serving or being served wine.

Selecting

Make a wine selection based on the occasion and the guest list. Follow with either the wine selection and then food choices or in the reverse order. There are preferred pairings of fruit and cheeses to accompany your wine selections.

Know there is a price and taste to fit every budget; however, don't base your purchase on price alone—celebrate in your unique style and preference.

Serving

Keep in mind when serving wines temperature matters. Before serving, decant red wine about an hour at room temperature; chill white and sparkling wines.

Enjoy the bubbles in bubbly—they are part of its fascination. Bubbles are formed in the second fermentation. Many hold to truth that smaller bubbles indicate quality.

Have appropriate glasses for the variety of wines you will serve. Stems are preferred.

> Red, a rounded bowl
>> White, a smaller tulip shape
>> Champagne, a flute

Keep a watch on your guest's glass to see that it stays filled.

Place your wine glass to the right of your water glass when setting the table.

Pouring

Pour wine, holding the bottle so guests can see the label.

Prevent dripping by twisting the bottle at the end of pouring a glass of wine and to give it a flourish. Some hold a small towel or napkin around the neck of the bottle. (Be especially careful when pouring red wines as the stain is difficult to remove if not attended to immediately.)

Fill a glass of wine as follows:

red wine 1/3 full

white wine 1/2 full

champagne 3/4 full

 Drinking

Enjoy wine by sipping, never gulping.

Hold a glass of white wine or sparkling wine by its stem to keep it cool; hold a red wine glass by the stem to appreciate the color and clarity of the wine and as well to keep smudges off the glass. Fingers can hold the bowl of a red wine glass. On all stem glasses, hold the stem between your thumb, forefinger, and middle finger. Other fingers rest naturally on the base of the glass. Look into your wine glass when sipping and not at your companion or another person.

Toasting

Toast to health, success, congratulations, happiness, or any other reason to celebrate a special occasion. Toasting is practiced around the world and from many centuries past.

Bring a first toast to a group as the host or hostess. Others may toast during the dessert or end of a meal.

The person making the toast usually stands and may invite the entire group to stand.

Enjoy being toasted but neither stand nor participate. Look pleased and humbly thank the group for the toast.

A last thought...
too much
of anything is, well,
too much.
Know when to
put a cork in it!

Salut! To Victor Robilio, whose passion for wine and history is evident in the five books he has authored: The Red Neck Guide to Wine Snobbery, Great American Guide to Fine Wines, Mighty Mississippi, The Way it Was, and Forever Young.

PET PEEVES OF
RESTAURANT SERVERS

*"The test of good manners is
to be patient with the bad ones."*
--Solomon Ibn Gabirol

When people asked me where I get the material for the radio shows, I say I just go to a public place and sit down for an hour or so. That is one hundred percent true when I am talking about dining manners. At times, I feel I have gone into a theater to watch a performance on "forgotten dining manners" rather than going into a restaurant and watching "real" people out for a "real" meal.

I wanted to interview a restaurant server to see if the

servers had "pet peeves" about diners just as customers have "pet peeves" about servers. A friend suggested her grandson, a fifteen-year server at a very popular local restaurant. I am so glad she did. Thanks, Tommie!

"Great service!"

Turns out, he had been a student in one of my classes at The University of Memphis. He must have finished the class satisfactorily as he agreed to be my guest. We had a fun conversation and I feel sure many of you reading this chapter will have to confess to some of the "peeves" he mentions.

I introduce you to James (JJ) Palmer. He prepared for the show by getting his co-servers in on the conversation and bringing a list to share with our listeners. Hopefully, their reminders will alert you to be more aware of dining courtesies at your favorite restaurants. JJ's list of servers' "pet peeves" is shown below.

This was a fun "assignment" and far easier than some of the assignments in your Business Communication class, Dr. Cherry. My co-workers and I picked behaviors that occur over and over. The customers, at times, seem to believe they are funny. I feel often times they just do not think about what they are saying or asking. For instance:

- A diner will ask what kind of beer we serve. When I tell him, he asks, "do you have XYZ?" I didn't mention XYZ because we don't serve it! You wonder if he was listening to what I said.

- Standard question. What is standard on your super burger? If I don't get onions, is it cheaper? I have to say "no."

- A diner comes in with a cell phone. Instead of reviewing the menu, the diner will engage in a cell conversation and then not be ready to place an order. The server has to come back, maybe several times. Finally, the diner is off the phone and asks the server, "Where have you been?"

- Again about cell phones…when a meal is finished, a diner may sit and talk on the phone while others are waiting for the table. Not very considerate of other diners nor of the server.

- Still another cell phone situation—a diner tries to motion the order with hand movements while talking on the phone. If you don't understand the hand motions and happen to get the order wrong, guess whose fault it seems to be!

"Waiter, could I have a glass of water?"

🍷 Diners who ask for salt. When I deliver, they ask for more lemon. When I deliver, they ask for an extra napkin, and so on. Wouldn't it be nice to hear all of these requests at one time?

Better for everyone.

🍷 Servers are not trained to answer to a diner's snapping. There are other ways of getting my attention that show more class.

🍷 It is so much easier to know that a group of diners wants to split the check *at the time they order* rather than *when they finish their meal*. (Just a "tip"…when this happens the server often comes out on the short end of their generosity.)

🍷 When diners have finished their meal (every last crumb) and then tell you it was not cooked as ordered. You know they may be fishing for a free meal. If mentioned earlier, the situation can be corrected very easily.

🍷 The best is saved for last. Grown-up diners who have forgotten the magic words: *Please and Thank you!*

Oh, and to answer Dr. Cherry's question. Yes, my experience over 15 years does bear out the fact that women, as a rule, do not tip as generously as men, especially when the men are accompanied by a very lovely lady. It is true, we are there to serve and to please our customers.

The philosophy in our restaurant is exactly that. I have

wonderful "regulars" (and I am always eager to meet and serve new customers) who allow me to enjoy coming to work every day. I am always happy to see them.

I love the sign I saw once:

There are more humans in this establishment than our customers. Thank you for treating us all with respect. Enjoy your meal.

Kindness and a smile will always count!

James (JJ) Palmer, a native Memphian, has spent over 25-years in the service industry and 18-years working at a locally-owned burger restaurant called Huey's. Although he earned his BBA from The University of Memphis, James soon realized that he got more satisfaction out of the relationships he built in the restaurant business. He definitely agrees…manners really do matter.

GUEST SERVICE
IN THE HOSPITALITY INDUSTRY

"Going the extra mile touches hands and hearts."
--Unknown

As travelers, we pick our lodging based on many factors: convenience, reputation, services offered, availability, pricing, purpose, and previous experience. We also travel for various reasons: fun, business, personal, education, and others.

We spread the word about our choices. We return primarily because of a good experience: Guest Service—the WOW factor.

In my experience, I have stayed in over-priced and under-rated facilities. Some demonstrating a frigid impression. Others greeting you with a warm smile and even a warm cookie. Whatever the reason—conference hotel for convenience, ocean-front for fun, or piggy-bank considerations—you are a guest and deserve quality service.

My guest was Britt Thompson, the Regional Director of Operations, Expotel Hospitality, LLC, in Louisiana. What I find most interesting in following Britt's career is his creativity in finding ways to deliver the WOW—ways to make his guests feel special. I asked him to comment on how my definition of manners—RESPECT—related to pleasing his guests. I like to think that just maybe some of my talk from "day 1" to "day now" found a place in his heart. Allow me to introduce you to my son, Britt, and his comments.

Each property has a distinct brand and personality. In every property where I participate in staff training, I use as a standard the belief that Guest Service begins with five simple Cs. This, of course, is not limited to hospitality; it extends to every successfully operating business.

👑 Competency

Every employee must know the services, products, and environment of the property. Know your brand. Know your management philosophy about service. Know your primary responsibilities yet also know that nothing the guest needs is outside your area of consideration—be thoroughly familiar with your resources and find a solution.

👑 Consistency

Treat guests the same every day, every call, every question, every encounter. Treat your managers, peers, subordinates, and vendors with equal respect. Bad days and disappointments happen yet they should not be a *"red-letter"* focus and never on display in elevators, walkways, or other public areas.

👑 Compassion

Get a feel for where your guests are coming from. If a group of athletes is using your property as a destination, use a sense of body language to feed your conversation. Is the team coming in after a high win or a disappointing loss? **Celebrate or Comfort.**

Complimentary refreshments on the ready in either situation. Not a part of any agreement. Just a touch of "a thoughtful thing to do." Respect—human to human.

 Comfort

Feel good in your own skin—in the service role you have. You won't accomplish this until you have respect for yourself. You can't extend what you don't possess. Be proud to earn recognition through achievements and demonstrate your accomplishments. Every employee represents the property brand. The image of every staff person portrays the image of your property brand.

 Communication

Listening, questioning, choice of words, tone of voice, and *an understanding and interpretation of non-verbal communication (body language).* These are all communication skills essential for excellent guest service—skills my mother taught me the importance of learning and practicing. It is important to remember there is never a time when we are not communicating—either to others or within ourselves.

Stay in touch.
  Follow-up.
    Did you earn their approval
    and respect?
      How can your services be
      improved?
        Will they tell others about
        your WOW service?
        Did excellence exceed expectation?

Most often we never know. When we do greet a guest for a return visit, you can bet the smile is genuine!

Every guest deserves the *5C treatment*—provide excellence that exceeds expectation. Display a natural smile every time you greet, welcome, or say "thank you" to a guest.

This is your statement of respect.

Stephen B. (Britt) Thompson *was Regional Director of Operations, Expotel Hospitality, LLC, Metairie, Louisiana. His 30-year career in the hospitality industry includes the San-Destin Beach Hilton in Florida and Ridges Resorts in Young Harris, Georgia. He enjoys golf and is a sports enthusiast.*

MANNERS FOR ROOMMATES

"Respect for ourselves guides our morals; respect for others guides our manners."

--Laurence Sterne

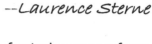

The topic for today came from two sources. The first—from remembering conversations of my son, grandsons, and their friends talking about experiences from dorm and frat house days. The second—from listening to my friends—most retired — talking about their decision to share a home with their children and family.

Many of the pleasures and frustrations expressed by these two groups were similar. Other co-dwelling situations might occur when adult children decide to stay at home early in their career or move "back home" after college to save a little money (and probably enjoy remembered conveniences). Two young people entering the workforce might want a living space other than what their budget can afford. These situations come with one question—how do I make it work?

I also think some newly married couples experience certain of these adjustments of co-dwelling. At times, I think about how nice it might be to have another human around to share conversations, offer opinions, share meals, and offer a cup of soup when I'm ill. Then, after thinking more about it, I dismiss the idea—at least for now. Whatever the reason for pursuing such a decision, enjoyable co-dwelling requires *effort* and *mutual respect* as a starting point.

I have been asked during presentations if I had suggestions to offer for "getting along" with a roommate. My best suggestions include:

- Making your list of the pros and cons of shared living.
- Having a serious conversation.
- Working out the differences and details.
- Putting the Agreement in writing.
- Thinking about it for a few days.

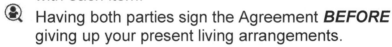

- Having a second conversation to be sure both agree with each item.
- Having both parties sign the Agreement **BEFORE** giving up your present living arrangements.

These steps should serve to determine if you are "good fits." (Personally, I would have the conversations over a meal to check out dining manners. I could not face poor table

manners at every shared meal.) To find sample templates, search "Roommate Agreements" on the internet.

My guests were Judy Burda and Doris Shumaker. Judy is my friend and co-author. Doris is her friend and neighbor. They both became co-dwellers recently with their daughters and sons-in-law. Below are their thoughts and suggestions from their experiences. Both admit to occasional "ups and downs" just as any two people might experience, relatives or not. Yet, both acknowledge the many positive points of their new home and living arrangement. Their comments are sure to give you plenty of food for thought.

🔍 *Respect and Consideration.* You will probably be seeing a lot of each other. There must be mutual respect—who you are and how you communicate. Are your behavior styles and morals compatible? Will your personalities be compatible?

🔍 *Space* (common and private). Look at your possessions. Check furniture and closet/shelf space. Is it adequate? Is it equal? Will you need to pare down in order not to spill outside your shelves, closets, cabinets, or storage space?

🔍 *Furnishings.* Blending shared furnishings is important as you decorate your home. Will the result be something you find comfortable and attractive?

🔍 *Finances.* Will you be able to meet your share of monthly expenses? Did you arrive at an equitable division of those expenses? Did you provide proof of this ability? Did you prepare a calendar of due dates that works well? Did you consider a "petty cash emergency fund" with repayment terms?

🔍 *Cleaning and other routine chores.* Did you both understand who will be responsible for general maintenance, food preparation, and clean up?

🔍 *Private time.* Do you have an understanding it is not to be considered rude if you go to your assigned room and close the door?

🔍 *Guests.* Did you determine who, when, and for what purpose guests will be joining you?

🔍 *Security and safety.* Are you in agreement with who will have keys and how security will be practiced for guests?

🔍 *Food and supplies.* Have you had a conversation about who purchases and pays for food—other than special, favorite items? Are there certain menu items to avoid either for taste or health?

🔍 *Mail and messages.* Is there a specific place to leave mail and messages? Is there an awareness that messages should be legible, complete, and confidential?

🔍 *Personal possessions.* Is there an understanding that possessions should not be borrowed without first asking and if borrowed, returned in the same condition?

🔍 *Help and assistance.* Will you be there for each other in the case of emergency to offer assistance when possible and if needed?

🔍 *Parking.* Is their comparable parking for both parties? If not, how will parking arrangement be determined?

🔍 *Pets.* If there is a pet involved, be sure everyone approves of pets, and no one is allergic to pet hair.

Also, there are pet maintenance and pet manners to consider.

The items listed are nothing more than behaviors of kindness—human to human—following the Golden Rule—
respect.

We both agree before an *item* becomes an issue—before either of us is *on our last nerve*, to have an open and honest conversation. Listen to each other and come up with possible solutions. Agree to give the best solution a try for a set period of time. Talk again. If this is workable, consider changing your Agreement. If not, and considering the severity of the disagreement, other solutions may be necessary. Life should be lived in peace, in personal happiness, and in appreciation of the rights and values of others.

Co-dwelling is an opportunity to practice good manners at their best!

Judith A. Burda, co-author

Doris Shumaker *followed a career path from Real Estate Broker, to hospital insurance/billing employee, to retirement, and crafting. She relocated to East Tennessee to co-dwell with her daughter and son-in-law. Her primary crafting boast is an Heirloom Wedding Quilt made from her wedding gown, which was also the gown worn by two of her daughters.*

Don't Forget Your Manners!

...In the Grocery and other
  Retail Stores

- Seize the moment to show consideration and manners while shopping.

- Park your shopping basket on either side of the aisle rather than in the middle when looking for an item. Spot a friend? Move to the end of an aisle or an open space to have a conversation—not in a congested area.

- Watch for moving shoppers when exiting the aisle.

- Remember, this is not the try-out place for loudest child with the shrillest lungs. Attend to your children.

- Read the signs for "quick check 15 items" and obey.

- Complete shopping *before* entering the check-out lane. Have coupons and shopping cards ready at the register.

- Check with Customer Service rather than the cashier when there is a problem or need for information.

- Do a good deed and allow someone with only one item to be checked out before you. (You'll feel great about it.)

- Be courteous to check-out personnel— they are standing all day and not just during rush periods. Share a smile with the baggers—they, too, are standing all day. (Yet, let them know not to turn the cake upside down or mash the bread!)

- Leave the building with caution and not poised to run people down when loading a car or crossing the lot. (At the same time, walkers should be "present" and alert.)

- Walk the cart to its designated parking spot rather than letting it roll across the lot and into a car or person.

MANNERS FOR THE GAY COMMUNITY

"Don't view marriage as between a gender and a gender—just between a spouse and a spouse."
--Unknown

We wake up in a different world every day.
    Laws change.
        Customs change.
            Environments change.
                People change their way of thinking and acting for personal reasons, business reasons, and sometimes just to make life easier.

Two Supreme Court rulings, The United States v Windsor which required the Federal Government to recognize marriage equality in 2013 and Obergefell v Hodges, which required states to recognize marriage equality in 2015, brought change to the gay community and as well to family, friends, associates, and the workplace. It brought happiness to couples who wanted their union to be recognized as legal. It brought questions to those wanting not to offend when extending invitations, addressing greeting cards, and business correspondence—and attending social functions, such as weddings and funerals.

I wanted to be able to answer questions asked out of respect and interest regarding manners within the gay community. Experience told me to go to the source—ask people who knew.

Following my own advice, I called a friend, Grant Whittle, who had helped me with projects through the years.

I invited Grant and his husband, Jimmy Hoxie, (who have celebrated their 6th anniversary) to be guests on my show. Being the gracious friends they are, they both agreed. They also agreed there were people, like me, with questions. We set the date.

In preparation for the show, I read a few books and a locally published magazine, *Focus*, to be able to express my questions clearly and come away with my needed information. The key topics: introductions, verbal and written communication, and other situations either wanted to share. I very much appreciated Jimmy and Grant's openness. Below are highlights of our conversation.

❤ Addressing a gay couple in writing

Addressing both individuals as "husband." (Example: in a newspaper wedding announcement, the wording: "Grant Whittle and his husband, Jimmy Hoxie, were honored at a reception celebrating their recent marriage…" *Note: in all examples, if this were a lesbian couple, "wife" would replace "husband."*

Addressing both individuals, again, as "husband" in an obituary. The wording: "Grant Whittle, who passed last week, leaves his husband, Jimmy Hoxie…"

❤ Addressing ourselves as a married couple offers choices:

Keep your surnames. (Jimmy Hoxie and Grant Whittle). This is the easiest and most popular.

Use both of your names. (Jimmy and Grant Hoxie-Whittle or Grant and Jimmy Whittle-Hoxie). There is no rule about whose name goes first. Most couples make the decision based on which sounds better.

Take your partner's name. (Grant Whittle and Jimmy Hoxie may become Grant and Jimmy Hoxie). This is usually preferred if there are children involved.

Choose a "new name" (Grant Whittle-Hoxie or Jimmy Hoxie-Whittle). This choice will require legal assistance and revisions on more documents.

Use the familiar and simple way for addressing two people who live together and who are not married: write each name on a separate line. The same works for a couple where the wife wants to keep her maiden name for professional reasons.

On legal documents, list and sign both names separately, or as they have decided to be recognized as a couple.

Grant and I decided to keep our names.

♥ Introductions

Janet, you already knew Grant. When we both saw you for the first time after our marriage, Grant said: "Janet, I want you to meet my husband, Jimmy Hoxie."

If you were introducing us as a couple to someone, you would say, "Bill, I want you to meet my friends, Grant Whittle and his husband, Jimmy Hoxie." This allows both of our names to be spoken to the person we are meeting. As well, you have stated that Grant and Jimmie are a couple and married. This offers clarification and is simply stated. *Note: If this were a lesbian couple, "wife" would replace "husband."*

♥ General Terminology

Words that, when used, do not downgrade or embarrass include: Orientation, Gay, Lesbian, Bisexual, and Straight. Words not suggested for conversation or writing include Gay (as a noun), Lifestyle, and Homosexual. There are other words heard on the street—usually voiced by people who do not approve of lesbian or gay couples—just as there are words that are not socially accepted for straight people. We feel such expressions should be kept to themselves.

♥ Social Occasions

Wedding ceremonies for same sex couples are not distinguishable from ceremonies for straight couples. Often wedding cake adornments show the figures dressed as same sex.

Table manners, place setting, or place cards show no differences.

Invitations and envelopes are printed/addressed as the couple's preference using both names.

♥ Travel

European destinations are more open to same-sex couples and show no discomfort if they are holding hands or share a kiss in public.

United States—New Orleans and New York are cities we travel regularly for vacation. We find these states follow the European comfort with same-sex couples.

United States—Our home state of Tennessee has taken longer to accept same sex unions and such symbols as hand holding in public. We think the feelings and acceptance are becoming more friendly.

♥ Other comments shared

Our families share holiday and vacation outings together and for the most part approve our marriage.

 One member is known as the grumpy person and although attends all functions has not openly accepted the marriage. As we noted in our conversation, even straight couples do not always please everyone with their choice of a life partner and life goes on in happiness for those who choose happiness.

There was a moment of apprehension when announcing wedding plans at our places of employment. This turned out not to be an issue. There is acceptance and joy for us among our colleagues.

What is in a person's heart and the respect shown to all human beings are where Grant and I are coming from. We live in peace and happiness and we wish all others the same.

Jimmy Hoxie is a chef and actor from Memphis, Tennessee. He enjoys gardening, making pottery, and travel. He never thought he'd find anyone to put up with his wide range of eccentricities and is thankful for his husband, Grant.

F. Grant Whittle is a web developer and language enthusiast from Memphis, Tennessee. He enjoys entertaining his friends at elaborate dinners and cocktail parties. He married Jimmy Hoxie in a simple ceremony in Washington, D.C., before it was legal in Tennessee. He has been much the better for it.

Don't Forget Your Manners!
...In Elevators and on Escalators

Follow the research for safety! Research shows the preferred way to ride an escalator is to stand still—don't walk up or down the stairs. If there is movement, the "unofficially preferred" method is to *stand* to the right and *walk* to the left.

Keep close control of children to avoid falls; no running on the stairs and hands held by a grown-up.

Avoid cell phone conversations in elevators and on escalators. This is not the place for cell phone use—general or personal.

Keep packages, shopping bags, and *large* handbags within your personal space.

Offer to punch a floor button for someone standing in the back of the elevator.

Remember your manners: "Please," "Thank You," "Excuse Me," when accidentally bumping into someone, stepping on a toe, or passing through a crowd.

DOG AND PUPPY MANNERS

"You'll never walk alone because I'll always be with you. Love, Your dog"

One day while still pondering a radio talk show, I sat down and began listing topics to cover. Puppy manners was high on my list. There has not been a pet in my home since we lost my son's dog who came to us when both were young. He and his Pierre were great pals. When my son left for college, Pierre grieved for months and protected his master's room with a vengeance. Their school break reunions warmed my heart.

Presently my association with puppies and dogs is during visits with my friends or when I happen to meet dogs walking their owners. Many of these occasions reinforced my wanting a conversation about puppy and dog manners. My search led me to the delightful Ann Marie Easton, owner of Pawsitive Companionship LLC, in Memphis. I enjoyed our conversation and learning about pet training tips, techniques, treats, and more.

Below are Ann Marie's suggestions and thoughts for enjoying your pets, allowing them to enjoy their world and family, have a trusting and respectful relationship with their owner, and charm friends and guests.

🐕 *Recognize* the earlier training begins with ownership of a pet, the more enjoyable and comfortable pets, owners, and guests will be.

Dog training begins with training the owner.

Remember puppies and dogs are much like people and need routines, manners, and love to allow everyone to live in harmony.

Recognize those good manners, neither in children nor pets, are learned at the time of need—for example, when company comes and the dog is barking, simply saying "hush" or "be quiet" is not going to accomplish anything other than a distraction for guests and confusion for the pet. Prepare for these occasions by training for quiet time and alone play time.

Determine how you want your pet to behave—what you want your dog to do (instead of not to do) and begin to train toward this behavior. The use of certain words will become cues for leading to the results you desire. What is learned will stay a lifetime.

Reinforce your dog's display of good manners routinely and especially when guests are expected. Teaching your dog to sit pretty and raise a paw when introduced to company will almost always result in making a friend of your guests—your friends will want to visit, and making owners proud as well. (An example is using a cue word such as "*introduce*" to trigger an extended paw as if to shake.)

Have a treat ready if company or family quiet time is needed. One very successful idea is to fill a Kong with your pet's favorite food. The Kong invites activity while holding the puppy's attention. After a while, the puppy will tire and is content to be in the room with everyone yet not a part of the conversation. Pets love the attention their human family gives them and, like children, don't like to share the spotlight.

🐾 *Reinforce* those behaviors you want your pet to do again in the future. If your pet is misbehaving, determine why so you can either ask your pet to perform an agreeable behavior or provide enrichment opportunities to expend the energy.

🐾 *Reinforce* good behavior and good habits with something (food, toy activity, or exercise) unique to the breed or your special pet.

🐾 *Allow* your pets to "speak" to you in assisting you to train them for feeding, exercise, and potty needs. Work with them to establish routines and comfort.

🐾 *Prepare* your dog for being alone. Having an abundance of attention and then being left alone may cause a change in behavior. Research does indicate that dogs may experience anxiety with sudden changes in surroundings or when humans they are accustomed to having near them are absent for periods of time. If long absences, such as work, may be a part of their life, prepare pets by having them experience short, frequent "alone time," building up to longer periods of time.

🐕 *Recognize* that your dog "reads" your body language and uses these "readings" as a kind of clock to learn regular routines. Changes in routines or in the environment could create apprehension and a behavior change.

🐕 *Keep* your pet's teeth clean and nails clipped. Our pets need medical and grooming attention just the same as humans. These practices are also signs of good doggy manners.

🐕 *Provide* variety in your pet's diet. Dogs get burned out on the same foods just as humans do. There are dozens of choices—even frozen food meals—offering taste and texture differences your pet will appreciate.

🐕 *Read* the labels of all food for your pets. There may be an ingredient in the food provided that could cause an upset tummy leading to lack of energy or restlessness. Check with your vet for best food options.

🐕 *Take* a cue from your pet to know whether a pet wardrobe is appreciated. There are many cute and tempting doggy accessories on the market. Most, of course, are for show.
However, rain gear and sweaters may be necessary on outdoor walks for some pets and can also make a "fashion statement," provided your pet enjoys showing off.

Learn the local leash laws. Respect the property of others and protect children, adults, and other animals.

Follow the wishes of your pets in showing manners by picking up after your pet while walking on public streets or private property.

Show your pet's appreciation to children who want to display kindness while giving attention to your puppy. Having your puppy sit while you supervise a child politely petting your puppy displays good manners to both a child and your pet. Be sure your puppy is at ease with a child's attention. We respect each other's personal space; we need to respect our dog's personal space. That is a sign of good manners.

> *In short, insist upon your pet's becoming a "manners' role model" for puppies and dogs.*

Well-mannered pets require much longer than a day's attention to learning, but patience reaps great rewards all around. Be patient! Be loving! There may be family members and friends who are not dog lovers. Yet, who's to know... your well-mannered pets just might change their attitude!

"My little dog—a heartbeat at my feet."
--Edith Wharton

__Ann Marie Easton__ is a Certified Professional Dog Trainer—Knowledge and Skills Assessed, a Pat Miller Certified Trainer, a supporting member of the International Association of Animal Behavior Consultants, a professional member of the Association of Professional Dog Trainers, and member of The Pet Professional Guild. She lives with her husband and three dogs.

Don't Forget Your Manners!
...At the Zoo

🐾 Count the animals at the zoo and you know you are in a very busy place. Then add the people—babies in buggies, youngsters in strollers, toddlers, teens, grown-ups, and seniors. Fun is the name of this venture and manners and fun are a team.

🐾 Abide by the rules and regulations established for both residents (the animals) and their guests (the public).

🐾 Keep personal equipment and belongings within the space provided on benches, tables, trams, and show seats in arenas.

🐾 Keep a trained eye on children. Children, stay with your group. Animals, clowns, balloons, and waterfalls may draw attention and often youngsters can go off in the blink of an eye. Little ones might think a swim with the seals or a romp with the pandas would be fun.

🐾 Listen to the zoo attendants as they instruct how to (or not to) feed and pet the animals. Don't decide on a new diet for the monkeys or birds. You don't want to make their tummies sick.

120

- Be patient when waiting in line for your turn to ride the ponies, train, or merry-go-round. Everyone is excited and anxious. No pushing ahead allowed.

- Find a container for your trash. Help keep the zoo clean for other visitors.

- Take pictures to remember your day at the zoo with all the lovely animals you visited. Most animals like to have their picture taken.

- Be sure to thank the zoo attendants, and of course, your parents, grandparents, or others who made this day happen.

Don't Forget Your Manners!
...At Fast Food Restaurants

- Remember, a fast food restaurant is referring to quicker service—not faster eating! Manners still apply.

- Keep elbows off the table.

- Place napkins in your lap and use them for face and fingers.

- Avoid cell phone conversations; be mindful of the people with you and enjoy your meal with them.

- Be considerate of those around you and keep your voice to a moderate volume.

- Help an establishment live up to its "fast food" name by being ready to order when your turn comes at the counter.

- Don't hold up the line by being on a cell phone.

- Thank the counter staff when your order is taken and when your meal is served to you.

- Keep your posture erect rather than slouching all over the booth. (Good posture is also good for digestion!)

- Keep feet out of the aisle to avoid tripping someone.

- Visit the restroom before you begin eating to wash your hands.

- Help yourself to the condiments you will use. Avoid being wasteful by taking more than you need.

- Clean up the table/booth you are using before leaving.

- Place trash in the proper containers and return trays to their proper place.

SCHOOL MANNERS

"Be present. Be creative. Be open-minded. Be positive. Be gracious."

--Judy Burda

School days, school days…every student will have something to recall about school day memories. Do you think if you picked a group of students today they could tell you what the 3 R's are? I tried it. The elementary students did not have a clue. Three of twenty college students answered correctly and shared a laugh—they had heard it from their grandparents. Here are the 3 R's from the song of the past: "Reading, and "R"iting, and "R"ithmatic. And, follows with "taught to the tune of a hickory stick!" Yes, a little out of touch for today's world. Still, reading, writing, and arithmetic are basic skills for every generation.

My show's producer, Dan Phillips, and I had a good conversation about school day memories: past and present. We agreed in today's world, there is strong evidence of something missing: we called the "something missing" manners. Yes, like listening, you do have to learn manners. Our show's conversation focus was school manners.

Reading + Writing + Arithmetic + Manners (respect)
= Life's path to
Acceptance + Self Esteem + Personal Success

We agreed to leave the reading, writing, and arithmetic to our teaching professionals. For our hour on the air, we focused on basic social skills benefiting and beginning with pre-school students and continuing well past college graduation. We encouraged parents listening (and you who are reading) to use our check points for parent-student conversations. It's a given that manners come primarily from home role models: parents. Yet, there are daily examples from pre-school to university classrooms making us ask, what's happening? Example: I live across the street from a respected public high school. Drivers dropping off and picking up students like to use our circle driveway as a quick turnaround. I and other condo owners attempted to stop this practice. We were told: "Get out of the way or I will run you down." And, "Here's to you, #@$*." And, "the finger." If these are the lessons modeled, no wonder road rage, bullying, school ground fighting, and classroom disrespect are leading to major community problems across the nation.

Disrespect is as contagious as respect! It attracts followers in public places, on educational campuses, in social gatherings, on the playing fields, in communities, and in families.

Dan and I offer the following tips to role models—parents and teachers--for teaching and demonstrating respect for self and students at all levels.

As *role models* ourselves, we invite you to join us: *read it, try it, share it, and model it.*

As *students*, we invite you to*: read it, soak it in, follow it, and share it.* The world needs more attention paid to the role good manners—*respect*—plays in interactions around the world—from youth to senior citizens.

Basics: *The Magic Words*
Begin with the basics: "Please," "Thank you," "Excuse me," "You are welcome," "I'm sorry." These basics

alone can defuse anger, promote comfort, express and acknowledge the value of others. An early start can become a lasting habit.

 ### *Body Language*

Our body movement—gesturing—says as much, if not more, than words. Good posture is a signal of self-respect which promotes respect for others. Your positive walking pattern reflects self-confidence—no shuffling— have a good, even stride.

 ### *Facial Expressions*

Although there are cultural differences to consider, a smile is acceptable and welcome in most cultures. A smile costs nothing but practice!

 ### *Appearance*

Your appearance will show your desire to be neat and fresh. Shirts in. Socks on. Shoe laces tied. Stress the importance of clean hands before and after eating, after bathroom stops, and before engaging in classroom activities. Cleanliness will attract others to you. Neatness will promote an organized mind.

 ### *Eating*

Use good table manners—don't embarrass yourself or others. Use a napkin. Elbows off the table. Don't talk or drink with your mouth full.

Don't take what others have—accept it if offered. Keep your eating space neat by cleaning up spills and throwing away trash. Dining manners will become a habit—make yours a good habit others will want to join.

 ### *Speaking*

Speak clearly and politely to everyone—parents, classmates, teachers, school staff, and guests—don't mumble. Don't interrupt others. Watch your language.

Follow School Rules

Know school rules and follow them—on the playground, in the parking lot, in the hallways, in the gym, in the cafeteria, in the library, in the auditorium, on the sports field, and in the classroom. *Know the rules as they apply to electronic equipment and to cell phones. Abide by them.*

Preparation

Have assignments ready on time. Get a good night's sleep, and get up early enough for a nourishing breakfast to enable full attention during class.

Transportation

Walking, riding a bike, sharing a ride, riding a bus, or driving a car all require respect and full attention to safety guides. Keep your eyes on the road to minimize distractions and accidents. As well, be a considerate and respectful passenger.

Respect

Show respect to everyone! Remember how YOU want to be treated and treat others in the same way. If you don't respect YOURSELF, you can't respect OTHERS. Compliment and congratulate your fellow students and teachers on accomplishments and recognition.

Be a Joiner, Contributor, and Volunteer

Learn to share your blessings, knowledge, time, and your heart. Join academic associations and volunteer for community projects. These opportunities will serve you a lifetime.

For sure there is an adjustment period for all first-year students: pre-school, first graders, freshmen— high school, and college. Parents and other role models, be there with  guidance. Don't underestimate the power of a smile, a kind word, a warm send-off in the mornings, and a listening ear in the evenings. An honest compliment, an encouraging word, or the smallest visible act of caring all have the potential to turn a life around or keep it headed in the right direction.

Throughout the years Dan has worked with youth as have I. We know the frustration and we know the personal rewards. We have worked with youth and adults in group situations— in Cub Scouts, in an orphanage self-esteem dance program, in summer community youth centers, in college classrooms, in mentoring new business owners, and in corporate offices sharing communication and etiquette instruction. If given the opportunity, most of the youth we have worked with express a desire to improve themselves in order to have a better chance of claiming *Satisfaction, Success, and Acceptance for themselves* in life. They just need to be given the tools and the time. There is a perfect place for each of us to share our expertise and concern— look for it and join in.

Let's find a way to make access to these basic skills of respect available to all of the young people and to role models as well within the community. Take the responsibility of role modeling seriously. Join Dan and me—together, we can make a difference.

Dr. Janet T. Cherry, co-author
Dan Phillips *is an actor and lover of the theatre and is a gardner whose efforts produce beautiful rose gardens. He is a radio producer who adds to the comfort and success of the shows' hosts under his care.*

Don't Forget Your Manners!
...With Quiz #3

1. Should you need to leave the table during dinner, place your napkin:
   a. To the left of your dinner plate.
   b. In the seat of your chair.

2. If your napkin falls to the floor:
   a. Pick it up, if it is accessible, and use it.
   b. Pick it up, if it is accessible, and ask the server for a clean one.

3. When you have finished your meal, place your napkin:
   a. Loosely folded and to the left of your dinner place.
   b. Folded up and placed in the center of your dinner plate.

4. Where do you place your cell phone on the table?
   a. To the right of your water glass.
   b. There is no place at the table for your cell phone.

5. When you need to attract the attention of the server:
   a. Hold your napkin up and wave to him/her.
   b. Catch eye contact or gently hold your hand just above the table.

(Answers on page 191)

Don't Forget Your Manners!
…In Theatres and in Movies

🎶 Be on time and in your seat BEFORE the play or movie begins.

🎶 Be courteous in allowing others to come past you if you are already seated.

🎶 Turn off or mute cell phone. (Hint…you could leave it in the car to avoid the temptation to use it.) Of course, no texting as the light is annoying in the darkened theatre.

🎶 Be seated in YOUR seat—if reservations are required.

🎶 Save conversation for before, intermission, or after.

🎶 Avoid giving away the plot.

🎶 Avoid crunching food wrappers—place wrappers in your pocket or handbag, not on the floor.

🎶 Keep feet on the floor and not pushed in the back of the seat in front of you.

🎶 No pictures of stage or screen action.

🎶 Please applaud to show appreciation to the performers.

🎶 Show courtesy when exiting the theatre *and* the parking lot.

Enjoy!

Don't Forget Your Manners!
...At the Fitness Center/Gym

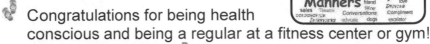

- Congratulations for being health conscious and being a regular at a fitness center or gym!

- Come to the center for its intended purpose: **fitness.**
- Dress appropriately. This is a place known for fitness: not fashion.
- Become familiar with the center's rules and follow them.
- Show extra consideration during busier hours. Be conscious of your time at a station. Don't hog the equipment.
- Know how to use equipment correctly before you decide to try it out. You do not want to injure yourself.

- Store your personal items in a locker, if available. *This is also a great place for your cell phone— turned off, of course.*
- Wipe machine handles and seats with a disposable cleaning tissue when you have finished with a set of exercises.
- Toss used tissues and other trash in the trash bin.
- Place used towels in appropriate containers.
- Ask for assistance only when the instructors are not engaged with another member.
- Put mats, weights, and other items back in their proper storage racks.
- Offer help if you see someone having difficulty trying to change equipment settings.
- Thank the attendants for their assistance.

SPORTS MANNERS

"Respect extends beyond the players to coaches, spectators, and officials."
--Britt Thompson

Manners travel within the world of sports—from peewee to national leagues.

Athletes display unique personalities and beliefs about their roles in their game of choice. From paid seats, free bleachers, field or court, RESPECT should be front and center. Rules of the sport will differ. There is still a common core of behaviors to acknowledge and honor.

My guest was Jake Thompson, a young sports reporter. He covers high school and university games and interviews the athletes and coaches—from season to season—sport to sport. He hears and watches from a front-row seat the style and sportsmanship on display. Jake's paper, *The Oxford Eagle,* refers to him as *a "sports fanatic."* I am very proud to refer to him as my grandson.

Here are his words and thoughts from our conversation.

I am proud of growing up with parents who were positive role models; my father and my grandfather were sports enthusiasts. Below are the behaviors of RESPECT that I notice, admire, and equate to "sports manners" both on and off the field in all athletic arenas. Additionally, every sport has its specific code of ethics and rules of the game.

 Recognition of team players with a sense of confidence and fairness. These players learn and grow through the encouragement and guidance of parents and coaches.

Role models prepare athletes of all ages to play the game with *respect* for both the winner and the loser in every contest.

Responsibility to learn the rules of the sport and abide by them.

Kindness in lending a helping hand to a player in trouble: team member or opponent.

Patriotism for our own Country or of the opponent to stand and remove helmet/cap for the playing of the national anthem.

Restraint not to throw equipment or demonstrate open disappointment or hostility at a call—perceived as fair or not—by the sport's official.

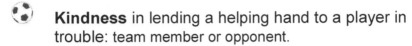

Awareness by spectators, parents, and fans that an admission ticket includes only a seat. It does not include the right to block views of others, shout obscenities, throw trash, or otherwise infringe on another's space.

Courtesy to give a solid handshake and a good word to the opponent after the game.

Thoughtfulness to congratulate players, coaches, officials, and fans on a game well played. Every player is out to do his/her best—neither to lose nor lose faith in the next scheduled contest.

Judgment to remember that both winning and losing are part of the game called sports.

P.S. Reporters should also show respect to coaches and players when questioning before, during half time, and following the game. They, too, should be respectful of both winner and loser.

Jake C. Thompson, *High School/Recruiting, The Oxford Eagle, Oxford, Mississippi, covers sports of three area high schools and The University of Mississippi (Ole Miss). He also is the host of a weekly radio talk show, Supertalk North Mississippi, in Oxford, Station 93.7.*

Don't Forget Your Manners!
...In Public Restrooms

Take note of the word "public." While there are stall doors for privacy in most public restrooms, the rest of the space is still considered a "public" space. Think before you act!

If there is a line, patiently wait your turn.

Close the door to the stall.

Use a toilet seat cover, if one is provided, and dispose of it before leaving. If covers are not available, wipe the seat when finished.

Leave unused toilet paper on the roll—and rolled up—rather than hanging off the roll and onto the floor.

Leave the toilet lid down.

Be sure to wash your hands! Wipe up splattered soap and water from the sink.

Do not use the common area for a dressing room. If a clothing change is necessary, use a private stall.

Use the diaper changing table, if provided, rather than the sink counter to take care of a little one's needs. Dispose of soiled diapers appropriately.

Do not forget a "tip" and a "thank you" if there is an attendant.

Do your part to leave the area as you would want to find it.

Remember, modesty and neatness show
respect for yourself and others.

CONDOMINIUM LIVING

*"Whether apartment, free-standing house,
or condo--it's home."*

--A. Grantham

How true it is! This quote should become a part of every condo contract as a reminder. First-time condo ownership is cause for living adjustments. And, it just might be some people are not cut out for multi-family communities.

I live in a small—31 unit—condo building. I have also lived in a 100+ unit property. I see little difference in owner behavior, cooperation, or communication. I served on my condo Board for six years (president for three) and I offer my *respect* and appreciation to any reader who steps up to volunteer for a Board position. *Respect and appreciation both demonstrate good manners.*

My guest was Mario Lara, a partner in Wright Property Management, Memphis, Tennessee. Wright manages 44 properties—some 2,900 units—with respect for each homeowner and his/her concerns. Below are Mario's reminders for showing respect for your co-owners while enjoying your home and maintenance-free living.

Whatever the design and style of your condominium property, *civility and respect* for your neighbors are expected and appreciated. Below are basic reminders.

Become aware of the property and its governing documents *before* you buy. If they are not compatible with your living style—continue looking.

▦ *Make* **an appointment** with the property management
team, or property Board when you
buy to schedule your move and to
allow you to get off to a good start
with your new neighbors.

▦ *Follow established security measures*. Knowing and
practicing approved security procedures shows that you
respect your neighbors and your community.

▦ *Comply with pet requirements, if pets
are allowed.* Home Owner Insurance
records confirm the largest number of
insurance claims involve pets. Pets are
"family" to the homeowner; however, not
everyone is a pet lover.

Clean up after your pet. Realize that
constant barking is annoying—even to pet lovers. *Follow
leash laws* for your property and city—outside your door,
on the elevator, and in the parking areas. (You might
also want to read the section in this book regarding *pet
manners*.)

▦ *Empty washers and dryers* to make them available for
the next user—a quick courtesy if there is a community
laundry.

▦ *Be mindful* of the appearance of common areas. You
own your unit: you also own a portion of common
property. While maintenance is provided, individuals
should not leave trash, furniture in disarray, display
unapproved personal decorations, plant shrubs/flowers,

use community kitchen for personal needs, post notices, or make other personal decisions regarding the common property areas.

🏢 *Keep noise levels in mind* when entertaining or just moving about in common areas or in your personal unit. Some buildings are more insulated than others and noise, especially during early or late hours, can be distracting.

🏢 *Follow pool and exercise room rules.* Both areas are intended for relaxation and enjoyment—be a contributor to that philosophy. Both areas have a need for safety, common thoughtfulness, and respect for others.

🏢 *Keep smells to yourself*— except maybe for outdoor BBQ grilling. Almost everyone is drawn to the wonderful flavors from the grill.

🏢 *Reach out* to help your neighbors in need. Just as important, know what NOT to do to avoid possible lawsuits.

🏢 **Use** your *assigned* parking space. Inside a garage is not the place to test your vehicle. *Stop, Look, Listen* for people and pets.

🏢 **Read** the governances, monthly Board minutes and other documentation intended to inform homeowners of important issues, events, and changes.

🏢 **Volunteer** for Board appointments and committee assignments. Your investment offers everyone the opportunity to be a part of the decisions and the management of your property. Everyone is needed!

🏢 **Show appreciation** for those homeowners who do volunteer for Board positions. *This is a volunteer responsibility protecting you and your property investment.*

**Remember, we all have the same
1440 minutes each day.**

🏢 **Be on alert** for unknown people and unwanted intrusions. Report as protocol states.

🏢 **Show appreciation** for your management team's employees—they enjoy hearing a "thank you" and a "job well done."

🏢 **Enjoy** your home, your neighbors, and your condo community.

🏢 ***Keep a friendly wave***, smile, and "hi" ready to brighten a neighbor's day. Offer your help. Don't forget a "please" or "thank you" for picking up mail, sharing a book, offering a taste or a recipe, or paying a compliment.

It only takes a second, and we have *86,400* of them each day.

Each of the statements listed above demonstrates in its own way—in many small ways—*neighborly respect*—*manners at their best!*

Wright Property Management and our employees attempt to share the above thoughts and manners' tips by example while working with Board members and the homeowners we serve at the properties we manage. We find these reminders go a long way in allowing all homeowners to find condo living friendly and satisfying.

Mario Lara *before founding Wright Property Management in 2005, with brother-in-law, Bob Noel, spent 35+ years in the hospitality and construction industries—Holiday Inns, SEFRA Management, and PCI. WPM takes great pride in defining its business model not only from an apartment management perspective, but also from an ownership viewpoint. A family owned business, WPM enjoys a great reputation in the industry and in the communities it serves.*

Don't Forget Your Manners!

...On Sidewalks

🐓 Be cautious with bikes and strollers.

🐓 Take charge of your four-paw friends. Keep them on a leash. Try not to annoy or frighten others.

🐓 Keep to the right when walking. Walking three or four abreast blocks passage of other walkers.

🐓 Keep your head out of your cellphone and eyes straight ahead for safety.

🐓 Show a smile when meeting walkers.

🐓 Please don't splash in a puddle!

...And in the Streets!

🐓 Obey the traffic signals, keeping motorists and YOU safe. Cross only at designated places.

🐓 Walk briskly so as not to get caught by a changing light.

🐓 Wave "thanks" to polite drivers if you are caught in the middle of the street.

🐓 Hold cell phone use until you are safely across the street. Cell phones are a distraction for walkers and drivers.

🐓 Be on the *alert* for drivers who aren't!

Be careful!

FUNERAL MANNERS

"Death leaves a heartache no one can heal.
Love leaves a memory no one can steal."
--from a headstone in Ireland

Life brings us in touch with many emotions. Our hearts may feel like bursting in joyful celebration or as easily want to shatter in pain and sorrow. Death is a part of life; it bears no exception. There are daily opportunities to express compassion and respect: *respect* is our guide. How we *show* respect will vary from occasion to occasion, culture to culture, religion to religion, and person to person. My quick advice when attending any funeral service is to avoid a razzle-dazzle appearance, leave the jingle bell jewelry at home, wear socks or hose to cover your feet, no flip-flops, and *definitely* no phone. Bring a listening ear and a warm heart.

My guest was Gregory (Greg) Griffin, Assistant Manager and Funeral Director, for Memorial Park Funeral Home and Cemetery in Memphis, Tennessee. Our conversation focused on the questions he is asked as part of his daily experiences when assisting with burial preparations. Below are his thoughts (and he also agreed with mine) on putting family, friends, associates, and visitors at ease when attending visitations, funerals, or memorial services.

The style of a funeral service most often follows the pattern of a person's life: culture, religion, family traditions, and daily lifestyle. This is how a person is known and will be remembered. Visitors want to pay their respects to the deceased with his familiarity and dignity in mind.

Key areas for consideration include the following:

 Visitations are normally less formal and precede the *funeral service. Memorial services* are held several days following the death and in lieu of a formal service. The local press is a primary source for death notices.

 Call the Funeral Home arranging the service or check the internet for **religious and cultural tradition,** if not familiar to

you. This could include floral selections, memorials, casket viewing, participation, and when to enter/exit the service—particularly if held in a church or synagogue. *Memorial* preferences are often included in the death notice. Florists can assist with color and flower choice based on cultural tradition.

 Show respect by being on time. If you arrive after the service has begun, do not draw attention to yourself when finding seating.

 Leave your cell phone in the car or turn it off. This is neither the time nor the place for placing or receiving a phone call.

 Dress for both men and women should be conservative—in good taste—what once would be termed as "church appropriate" (suit/jacket and tie for men; dress/pantsuit for women).

Neither jeans nor sports clothing is considered appropriate. *Note:* If a man is serving as a pallbearer, a dark suit, white shirt, and tie are expected.

Consider the relationship, age, and behavior of children when making a decision about their attending a funeral. *Note:* Many funeral homes have a special area where children will be comfortable and cared for during the service.

The same decisions apply to *pets*. Pets, if well behaved, commonly attend visitations—especially if the pet is a service animal. Pets tend to calm a grieving family. Remember, animals grieve when a member of their family is missing. Being with family also calms their emotions. (See the section in this book on *Pet Manners*.)

Express your feelings...What to Say? What Not to Say? You are there to comfort the family and loved ones of the deceased. Tell a story (it *can* be funny— and *should* be short) about a connection between you and the departed. Praise by example positive achievements, acts of kindness, willingness to help, competitive and creative skills you shared, and why he/she was your friend, coach, mentor, co-worker, or volunteer partner.

Your interactions may not be familiar to friends or family and it is a comfort to hear them. Be genuine and expressive. Preparing yourself for this conversation always enables a smooth delivery. It helps to avoid "foot in mouth" embarrassment with questions concerning the death, the pain, or the hardships.

Be a good listener. It is comforting to those left behind to talk about their loved one.

143

 **Sign the Guest Register** so later the family is reminded of who attended.

 **Honor the family by attending a reception,** if held, following the service. An invitation is usually extended at the conclusion of the service.

 **Follow-up cards and calls are always a thoughtful gesture.** Food is also appreciated. For ease in planning gifts of food from a group, visit ***www.takethemameal.com***.

The most important etiquette rule to remember is to treat those in mourning with kindness, warmth, love, and respect.

When a family member or close friend experiences a loss, reach out and provide support. Nobody should have to experience bereavement alone. You always have a friend at your funeral home. We want you to be comfortable in knowing we care.

Gregory J. Griffin is a native Memphian and an Assistant Manager and Funeral Director at Memorial Park Funeral Home and Cemetery in Memphis, Tennessee. He has degrees from Mississippi State University and The University of Memphis. Gregory is married to Natasha and has two daughters, Hadley and Eliana.

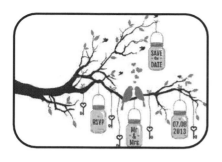

POP-UP EVENTS

"At first, they will ask why you're doing it. Later they'll ask how you did it!"
--Author Unknown

Always searching for radio program ideas, I came across an advertisement in the local *Memphis* magazine inviting people to attend a pop-up charity wedding event. It intrigued me. I called to ask questions and the more I heard, the more interested I became. Turns out, pop-up events are gaining recognition and popularity across the country. From what I gathered, pop-up events are "seemingly" spontaneous yet "perfectly planned." That sounds like quite a challenge and a grand accomplishment.

My call paid off. While I learned about the pop-up entertaining trend, I also met Betsy McKay, the Director of Sales for The Cadre Building, a historic and elegant landmark in Memphis. The Cadre Building is beautifully appointed in design and décor for both large and small events. Betsy also heads **Salt Style and Events,** her own event planning company—celebrating its fifth year. Our conversation focused on just what pop-up events entail. We talked about a pop-up wedding and how traditional wedding manners apply to this developing trend. Below are her thoughts and suggestions for considering a pop-up event.

Pop-Up Entertaining

The trend of pop-up entertaining came into full focus about a decade ago. Pop-up entertaining can be chosen for any type of function, and the location can be as varied as the event. Creativity is always a factor in event planning and certainly this is true for pop-up preparations. Certain points I focus on with clients are:

- Dates, Time, and Cost

Always adding the caution…*it is never too early to begin planning!*

Thinking through the event planning categories can be mind-boggling. There are considerations for:

- *Location* (formal, rustic, seaside, mountains, indoors, outdoors)
- *Food* (formal seated, brunch, casual, cookout, appetizers only, dessert only, wedding cake only, cookies only, or many other options)

- *Clothing* (white tie, black tie, traditional wedding, or casual)
- *Invitations/announcements* (designed, printed, shelf)
- *Music* (live, recorded, DJ, individual instrumental)
- *Flowers* (live, silk, individual to large arrangements)
- *Miscellaneous expenses*
- *Lodging and transportation*

Coordination can be difficult. This in itself is a justifiable reason for looking at a simpler and less stressful plan.

Traditional or Pop-Up?

There are many reasons pop-up events are chosen. Some of the most often stated by clients I have worked with are: limited time, space, and resources. Sometimes there are too many people to please with decisions, surprise appeal, simplicity, and budget concerns. Some pop-up affairs are planned with a

 surprise in mind for those attending. For instance, invitations may be for dinner. After the dinner you are told, "Oh, by the way, we are happy to have you here to attend our wedding."

 Manners Always Matter

Whether the decision is traditional or impromptu, courtesy and respect should be shown to those directly involved: family members, guests, and vendors. Etiquette considerations include:

- Selecting the design and proper wording for invitations/announcements.
- Addressing invitations properly.
- Including a response card (and for weddings, after ceremony address card).
- Having appropriate table settings for formal, seated meals, and buffets.
- Serving selections for beverages before and after the main meal.
- Toasting: if, who, when, what to say.
- Sending properly written thank you notes in a timely manner to appropriate people for gifts, services, and special favors.

An event planner is the master coordinator; however, vendors may also assist with appropriate etiquette checks within their area of expertise. Cultural differences may require special attention and consideration. These may include choice and color of flowers, food and beverage selections, table settings, and even the ceremony itself.

Pop-Up Opportunities

Pop-up events are not limited to weddings. The excitement of a non-traditional affair of any kind—from retail to seaside dining—can give a twist and a pop to gatherings intended for fun, the sun, profit or charity--each as unique to the purpose and personality of the host/hostess.

A pop-up wedding will provide loving and happy memories of a special kind. Other seemingly spontaneous events draw attention to retail and bring awareness and new appeal to products, services, and people.

Interesting choices await to create your dream affair. Whatever your decisions, create happy memories.

Betsy Comella McKay is the owner of Salt Style & Events, a full-service event planning and design company. Born and raised in the South, Betsy says she owes her creative instincts to her mother and grandmothers who inspired a passion for entertaining. Betsy's attention to detail and her ability to showcase her clients' personalities leave a lasting impression.

SALES MANNERS

"Remember not only to say the right thing in the right place, but far more difficult still, to leave unsaid the wrong thing at the tempting moment."
--Benjamin Franklin

The title "sales profession" represents a vast number of individuals. While the products and services are quite diverse, the strategy for success is not all that different according to my research. Probably all of us have had experiences where we wondered if the person representing the seller realized what exactly their position entailed. The second annoying treatment in a sales situation, for me, is to realize that I know more about a product than the sales "professional," and I came in with questions!!!

My guest was Mary Sharp. Mary is a Real Estate Broker with 31 years in the profession. She has proudly earned the title "Realtor® of the Year" from the Realtor® Association. I met Mary through a mutual friend, also a Realtor®, who had recommended me to work with the Memphis Area Association of Realtors® (MAAR) on a new program being introduced in the Memphis market. I thought of Mary immediately for the radio show remembering my "first impression" of her, as an individual and as a professional, her approach to sales, her interaction with her associates, and her tag line, "Always Follow the Agent Who Cares."

Below Mary shares her sales philosophy and how it all begins and ends with manners.

My focus is on both buyer and seller and I have tried to embrace this focus for the 31 years I have been in real estate. There are, of course, transfer skills brought with you from profession to profession. However, there are also skills that must be learned and imprinted in your life for a particular market—such as real estate.

I started with myself, and my basic professional attire. I decided on a suit, white blouse, lapel flower, and comfortable dress shoes. My mirror approved and agreed I looked "professional."

My second step toward being "realtor ready" was the understanding that I had to be knowledge ready. Yes, I had passed all of the required examinations. Now I had to be ready to apply that knowledge—and stay up-to-date.

I needed the appropriate questions ready for clients—and to do this I needed to *know how to listen.*

I also needed to have the answers to their questions—and to do this I had to *know more about questioning.*

I am a believer in the high stakes *listening* plays in sales. When you lose a few sales because of poor listening skills, (this happened to me) you take note and learn more about this important communication skill. As Janet and I talked on the show, listening is a learned skill. I encourage those new to the realtor ranks to learn to listen—and to question. (*You might want to take a look at two other chapters*

in this book: "Listening" and "Questioning" for great tips.)
Realtors have a Code of Ethics. The first statement is The Golden Rule.

Do Unto Others As You Would Have Them Do Unto You.

This statement embraces the basic definition of manners: *Respect*. Respect for yourself first, which allows respect for others.

Other "personal and professional" rules I stand behind are:

 Tell people only what you know rather than what you "think" you know.

 Appreciate cultural differences.

 Avoid terms of endearment (honey, sweetie, etc.).

Turn cell phones off when with a client. You owe your attention to the person in front of you.

Other statements from Realtors' Codes:

 Be on time for all appointments. In fact, be 5- to 10-minutes early to check everything out prior to time to meet your client.

 Greet with a smile and handshake. Make it a genuine smile and a firm handshake. Remember, if words and body movements are not congruent, the belief is most often in the non-verbal expression.

 Speak your client's name. Be sure to have the correct pronunciation. If unsure, ask.

Communicate with all parties. Make it a habit to be sure all persons involved know and agree on time, place, and other important facts. (Just to be on the safe side, always announce yourself as you enter a home.)

Respect your fellow Realtors/competitors. This is true for both written and spoken conversation and information.

Promise only what you can deliver. This is not only professional, it stands out not only with your clients; it brings referrals.

Stay connected. Follow-up. Check on a person out of concern or with additional information—yet, don't become a pest!

Remain enthusiastic! Positive energy is contagious.

Thank you. These words should end every communication, conversation, and in-person meeting.

In summary:
　Be Golden,
　　Be patient,
　　　Be aware,
　　　　Be educated,
　　　　　Be energetic,
　　　　　　Be enthusiastic,
　　　　　　　Be ethical!

Mary W. Sharp has been a REALTOR® for 32 years with various companies, and is licensed in Tennessee and Mississippi. She loves helping buyers and sellers with their most expensive asset—a Dream Home. Mary was chosen as REALTOR® OF THE YEAR, for Memphis Area Association of REALTORS® in 2010.

DRIVING MANNERS

"Skillful driving is not defined by straight roads."

--William King

If you are a driver, a passenger, or parent of a driver, you might have wished at one time or another, as I have, that all people sitting behind steering wheels had more appreciation and respect for vehicles and pedestrians. Along with that, a realization of the potential damage an average 4,079 lb. vehicle they are driving can do (quoted from E.P.A. weight statistics).

You might join thousands, including me, who wish for more respect and patience from drivers. You might also wish drivers exercised more caution and courtesy when on our streets and highways. Yes, it is necessary to display a certain amount of knowledge of the rules, regulations, and laws governing the right to hold a valid driver's license. This, however, is not always enough to prevent costly accidents and deadly results.

Driving is another area of life where manners play a role. As I mentioned every Saturday morning on my radio show, manners go with us wherever we go—and this is true whether we are driving a car, riding a bicycle or motorbike, walking, or trusting someone else to get us safely to our destination.

I wanted to call motorists' attention to driving safety. My research led me to Pitner Driving Education. Mr. Pitner was most cooperative and found a way to fit the show into his very busy schedule. I was blown away by the number of students Pitner enrolls and impressed with the recognition on their website of the achievements of their student drivers. I feel the more our young people—all want-to-be drivers actually—learn about proper driving techniques, rules, and laws the better.

My guest was Keith Wiley, a Pitner Driving Education Instructor. Keith shares important tips about driving safely and courteously.

Just as Janet was happy to find us, we were equally pleased to have another outlet to reach motorists and to remind them to form and follow safe driving habits.

Our city has heavily traveled streets and roads. There will be

accidents. Many of these accidents could be avoided by keeping our eyes on the road and our minds tuned to the task at hand: safe driving and showing respect to our fellow motorists and pedestrians.

There could be a very long list of tips to share. Keeping in mind we had only an hour, my list will focus on what I, and others in driver education, consider highly important to attempt to avoid accidents.

Keep your car in top repair and running condition. When a car malfunctions, it is distracting and stressful to the driver. Be weather ready with working windshield wipers and defroster.

Avoid operating distracting "gadgets" when driving. **The cell phone is a top distractor.** Use while driving is against the law in many states. If you need to make or receive a call, pull off the street. (Surveys have found cell phones and tailgating to be the most annoying driver practices.)

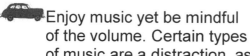Enjoy music yet be mindful of the volume. Certain types of music are a distraction, as is a high volume.

Be attentive to traffic lights. Red and green signals are there to keep traffic flowing safely. Regard the yellow caution as a slowing down guide rather than a signal to speed up. Also watch for and obey speed limit postings.

See that a friend's car starts before driving away.

Should you see the flashing lights of a Traffic Officer

behind you, then is the time to show patience and politeness. Show your license, proof of insurance, and listen to the officer. You might also call 911 to see if the stop is legitimate before sharing your information.

Use your authority as the vehicle driver to request passengers in your car to buckle up and use good communication judgment so as not to distract the driver.

Make kindness a habit. Allow drivers stuck in traffic or behind a stalled vehicle to move into your lane. At the same time, if you are the receiver of such a kindness, show your appreciation with a wave to the driver. This simple gesture gives a "good feeling" to another person and perhaps it creates a "pass it forward" kindness.

Keep in mind that public parking spaces have lines to assist you in parking correctly. Use only one space and pull all the way in to allow convenience to another driver. Also, give drivers necessary time and space to back out.

Drive slowly and defensively in a parking lot or garage. Pay attention to pedestrians—senior citizens, stray children, handicapped individuals, and pets. Don't rush them. Don't honk at them. Save your horn for avoiding accidents. Follow the markings and arrows on the lot or in the garage. Watch out for stray shopping carts.

Avoid road rage when possible. Keep cool. Allow the distressed driver to move on. Road rage often leads to more dangerous and unsafe situations.

Give yourself extra time to get to your destination without being stressed or frustrated with traffic.

Do not drive while eating. Managing food and beverage while driving is unsafe. Drive-in diners have plenty of space to park and eat.

Pay attention to and abide by turn lanes and turn light signals. Always signal when you are changing lanes.

 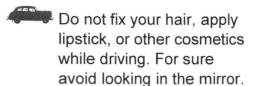 Do not fix your hair, apply lipstick, or other cosmetics while driving. For sure avoid looking in the mirror.

Remember polite drivers do not park in a handicapped space. Nor do they litter.

Keep a safe distance from the car ahead of you should the car stop suddenly.

If you are involved in damaging another car, do the proper thing and leave a note with your contact information on the car under the windshield wiper blade.

Driving with good manners makes everyone's journey more enjoyable, stress-free, and safer. The best part, courtesy costs nothing. It's a good habit to practice—try it.

Keith Wiley has taught Driver Education at Pitner Driving School, Inc. since 2007. He is the father of three good, conscientious drivers. Pitner Driving School, Inc. has been proudly teaching comprehensive defensive driving skills to high school students and adults in the Memphis, Tennessee, area since 1979.

Don't Forget Your Manners!

...At the Buffet

Enter the buffet line after you have checked where dinnerware and utensils are located. Also, check the food items so you can plan your meal.

Use the serving utensil for only one dish and return it after serving yourself.

Do not reach across or over another person while serving yourself.

Remember you can return to the serving line as many times as you wish. It is neither polite nor necessary to see how much food you can fit on your plate.

Think in terms of courses: appetizer, soup, salad, entrée, dessert. Consider a separate trip to the buffet table for each course.

Keep the line moving. There may be people behind you waiting to be served. Fill plates for children.

Follow guidelines for dining etiquette (use of utensils, napkin, glassware). Buffet line etiquette is the same as for any seated meal.

Remember for each visit to the buffet line you should serve yourself on a clean plate. Leave your used plate for the server to remove from the table.

Return to the table and begin eating. It is not necessary to wait for every person at your table to be served. Since people do return for seconds, this could get complicated.

Do not ask for a "doggie bag."

If you don't like something, just leave it on your plate.

THE BREAK-UP

"Even finding and tasting the porridge that is 'just right' doesn't guarantee a wonderful breakfast."
--Dr. Janet T. Cherry

Goldilocks had the right idea—you don't know when you have something that is "just right" until you have sampled others. And, that goes for more than just porridge, chairs, and beds. If you have not read *Goldilocks and the Three Bears* in a while, you might enjoy it again. Finding the "just right" relationship may well be the task that can take a lifetime. Those who are blessed with the right choice early in life should say a "Thank you, Lord" every night, and a "Thank you, my friend" to your partner every day.

Happy and lasting relationships can be the sweetest of life's gifts. However, they often seem no more predictable than the weather. Meteorologists, though sometimes wrong, do forecast a storm is coming before it hits. Unfortunationately, love is said to be blind and the signs are missed. Caring seems to end on a whim, without a clue, cold and brash, time together not considered, some ending decently, most not.

How to handle a relationship break-up with poise, dignity, and yes, manners, was far from my list of radio show topics. Life had been kind in recent years so I chose to leave the topic to magazines and movies. That was two years ago. Time has changed my mind.

The heart is tender, complicated, and vital to life. A break-up is stressful for both parties involved and should not create a potential health crisis. True, the dumpee usually does bear the brunt of hurt and stress to a greater degree. If a break-up is something you feel must be done, please consider the points below to keep appreciation of past times together as guidelines for final conversations.

- Have this conversation in person unless distance makes it prohibitive. This is not the time for text messages, emails, or phone calls.

- Avoid dates of celebration: birthdays, holidays, anniversaries, or other dates of special significance.

- Find an appropriate and private location.

- Be prepared with what you want to say—and say it.

- Speak with kindness.

- Refrain from anger, blame, and harsh facial expressions.

- State the truth no matter if it will be painful to say—or to hear. The truth is deserved however shocking or painful it may be.

- Listen to and answer questions truthfully as they may arise.

- Remember there has been a history between you—the longer the time the more this conversation can hurt.

- Thank this special person for the many positive and happy moments that were shared.

- Apologize for the pain you feel this is causing.

- Select a time to finalize personal matters and possessions.

- 💔 Suggest how you feel future conversations, functions, and feelings should be displayed.

- 💔 Offer an adult-level and appropriate closure.

- 💔 Express a good-bye in a manner you feel the past calls for: an embrace, a hug, a handshake, or nothing at all.

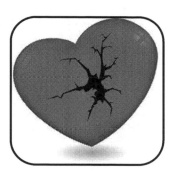

- 💔 Walk through the door and let it close. If this person is so eager to walk away from you, don't stop him/her. Be strong enough to let it happen.

- 💔 Deal with your emotions in private.

Post-breakup behavior

- 💗 Be civil—exchange a greeting when confronted.

- 💗 Be consistent in your behavior. Don't complicate issues. If conditions exist that compel you to see each other (office or neighborhood) on a regular basis, again, be civil.

- 💗 Try to establish some type of friendship. This could happen over time.

- 💗 Respect this person for who he/she is.

- 💗 Refrain from negative comments and/or actions.

Recovery from a break-up is not easy. Dignity is bruised.

 After the door is closed and single life begins again, or at least for the person dumped, time takes a pause. Life takes a pause. Avoid allowing stress and sadness to weigh physically on your heart. Replace the stress with new options, new choices, a new adventure, and continued good health practices.

For readers who may be going through a break-up, consider these suggestions for recovery:

♥ Allow a short time to wallow, feel alone, and live in the "pity-poor-me" syndrome. You deserve that time—make it short.

♥ Thank the person who shared information about an infidelity and kept you from a potentially unbearable and embarrassing situation (Also, keep this person anonymous.)

♥ Sort through your remembrances and keep only those you cherish for the item itself—not for the person who gave it to you.

♥ Start a search for creating newness in your life: adventure, creativity, new places, and new people. Expose yourself to new sounds, new books, and join a fitness center. Learn to play the piano, join a choir, volunteer, or even write a book!

♥ Make a contract with yourself to start and complete something very special to you in your life that will make you feel whole and new again, competent, accomplished, and will provide a positiveness for others.

♥ Have a huge celebration once your contract is fulfilled.

♥ Lastly, send a copy of this book to:

- The person who needs to know good manners for his/her next break-up.
- A person you know who doesn't deserve going through misery because of a break-up. (You could purchase a copy of this book for your friend.)

♥YOU CAN DO THIS!

Remember, Goldilocks ran out of the house and into the woods when she met the three bears.

You have the courage to stay,
face the situation,
and conquer.

My best to you!

Dr. Janet T. Cherry, Author

Don't Forget Your Manners!
...In Languages

Please and Thank You,
And a "Hello" for good measure!

Language	Please	Thank You
Spanish	Por favor	Gracias
French	**S'il vous plait**	**Merci**
German	Bitte	Danke
Italian	**Per favore**	**Grazie**
Mandarin	Qing	Xièxiè
English	**Please**	**Thank You**
	(or in the South: Thanks, y'all)	

Language	Hello
Spanish	Hola
French	**Bonjour**
German	Hallo or Guten Tag
Italian	**Ciao**
Mandarin	Ni Hau
English	**Hello (or in the South: Hey, y'all)**

The languages shown above all fall within the top 20 most widely spoken in the world. The internet offers many more languages for you to use in representing yourself and when addressing Internationals.

CHECKLIST FOR INTERNATIONAL TRAVEL

"The greatest moment in human life is
a departure into unknown lands."
--Lucy Benson

Travel continues to fascinate the curious and adventurous. Visiting a new destination, especially an international location, for whatever reason, seems to rally excitement. If you are preparing for international travel, the preparation

should also include equal attention to the cultural differences depending upon your destination. I find international etiquette and customs equally as fascinating as the historical landmarks and the unique offerings in music and art. Visitors to distant places are immediately labeled—consciously or unconsciously—as ambassadors for ourselves, our employer, our organization/association, and our country. Certainly, we want to make a positive first impression whether we are on a social visit, a business transaction, or making a formal presentation at a conference—just as individuals do when visiting the United States. Preparation is essential.

My guest for this show was Dr. Lillian Hunt Chaney, the co-author of books on international etiquette and communication. Our conversation was fun and informative. We reviewed an International Travel  Checklist she prepared. Below are just some of the items worth noting when preparing for international travel that we covered in our one-hour program.

✈ Greetings

Depending on the part of the world you are visiting, the most common types of greetings are the handshake, bow, kiss, and/or hug.

Following the local customs is recommended when greeting individuals. It shows respect. Even handshakes differ among cultures. In the United States, we offer a firm, yet not crushing, handshake, along with direct eye contact as we greet someone.

✈ Introductions

Introductions show respect. In the United States, introductions are made showing respect for age, title, and gender.

Introductions may also follow a more casual protocol. As an example: "Jean Brown, I want you to meet Joe Cotton." This is acceptable in an informal chance meeting.

Whatever the cultural preference, the important thing about introductions is to remember to make them.

✈ Business Cards

Have a good supply of business cards and keep them "fresh" by using a card case.

Print the back of your cards in the language of the country you are visiting.

Present your card in a position allowing the recipient to read it as handed to him/her.

Show respect for the card and its presenter by not placing it in your pocket without reading it or writing notes on it (at least not until you have departed). Be aware of card and print colors.

✈ Dress

Select conservative attire—whether for casual, business, or social activities.

Think about travel clothing which in general is much more casual. Should you and your luggage become separated, you will want at least one outfit available for general occasions. Bone up on the color protocol in your destination. For example, bright colors are not preferred in Belgium.

Select shoes for comfort based on known activities.

Do not try to follow the typical fashion of a country. Of course, T-shirts and other local items are fun to wear as appropriate for the occasion.

✈ Gestures

The meaning of body language also differs from country to country—especially eye, facial, hands and feet expressions, and movement. In Japan prolonged direct eye contact is considered impolite or even intimidating; in the Orient direct eye contact is not favored, whereas in

America, we feel direct eye contact indicates attention and good manners.

The "OK" gesture, recognized as American-born, means "Everything is fine." or "Everything is OK." In France it means "zero" or "worthless," and in Japan it is the signal for "money."

In many parts of the Middle and the Far East, showing the sole of your shoe sends a rude message.

In most parts of the world, a smile is recognized as an expression of kindness and acceptance.

✈ Dining Etiquette – Continental vs American

Know the differences between Continental and American style dining. This will include placement of your dining utensils, the order in which the courses are served, and how to hold your knife and fork when cutting and eating meat and vegetables.

Use your utensils from the *outside in* as they are placed on the table and to the left and right of your dinner plate.

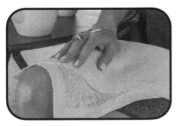

Place your napkin in your lap, as opposed to in your shirt collar or not using it at all. Your napkin may be found to the *left* of your dinner plate, in the middle of your plate, or inside your water glass. Should you leave your seat prior to finishing your meal, place your napkin in your seat as this will alert the server that you will return. If you have finished your meal, loosely fold—not wad—the napkin and place it to the left of your dinner plate. This alerts the server you will not return.

✈ Space

Every culture has its "space" protocol. The United States has four space zones: intimate, personal, social, and public. And, while we are considered a "no touching" society, hugs are common among family and friends.

✈ Time

Be aware of how promptness and lateness are treated within your destination—particularly in business. If you are visiting a culture where promptness is the rule, being even five minutes late will often influence business decisions.

✈ Color

Color has a language all its own. This applies to products, print, flowers, gifts, wrapping paper/bows, and in certain instances clothing. As with the earlier mentioned categories, it is best to check a reputable guide on international behaviors and customs.

✈ Verbal (oral) Communication – Formal and Informal

 Learn a few words in the native language. People will understand that you may not speak their language fluently. They will appreciate you for your efforts in at least knowing words such as "hello," "goodbye," "please," and "thank you." The more, the better.

Know also to refrain from using jargon or slang.

Do not chat with others in a language where one or more persons will not understand.

✈ Humor

Humor is often heard through the listener's perspective. The interpretation might be based on cultural factors, and for this reason, one should be very cautious—perhaps avoiding the use of humor altogether.

We have only touched the surface of this topic. I strongly recommend an investment in a book or two on international protocol and the specific country you plan to visit. Maybe this would even be good reading material on the flight.

"Travel makes one modest. You see what a tiny place you occupy in the world."

--Gustave Flaubert

Dr. Lillian H. Chaney *was a Distinguished Professor of Office Management and Professor of Management at The University of Memphis for many years. She co-authored six books and over 100 articles in professional journals, in addition to conducting seminars for corporate and professional groups. Her awards include the University's Distinguished Teaching Award.*

CUBA TRAVEL

*"We travel not to escape life,
but for life not to escape us."
--Anonymous*

The idea for this Saturday morning's conversation was part inspiration from my friend, fellow trainer, and professional photographer extraordinaire, Jeanne Baer, and part nostalgia from my travels with my father to Cuba in the late '50s. My last trip with him was in 1956 and on January 1, 1959, Castro took control. American travel and my father's business both came to an end. Although there are times when I can't remember what I did yesterday, my memories are quite vivid of Havana's attractions and natural beauty.

It was both interesting and sad to hear Jeanne talk about present conditions. My hope is Havana will be a "come-back-kid" before long and more Americans will fully enjoy the island and its treasures. Cuba is already becoming a favorite new destination for Americans. Travel

restrictions are changing quickly and I feel Cuba will be added to our list of international destinations. When this happens visitors will want to prepare and respect cultural differences.

I asked Jeanne to tell about the Cuba she found two years ago, to update me and American travelers on present-day Havana, and how to interact with its citizens. Would I return? I think not. I would rather remember it as I found it in the '50s.

Below are Jeanne's impressions and comments from her visit to Cuba.

## People and Education

Cuban people are charming, educated, friendly, energetic, ambitious, and eager to chat with tourists. They happily pose for pictures and engage in conversation.

Americans are not as familiar with the Cuban population and its customs as Cubans are familiar with Americans and American customs. Almost every Cuban has acquaintances and/or family in the U.S.

Education is free and provided by the Government through the university level. The universities graduate high numbers of professionals, particularly with education and medical degrees. Doctors are frequently sent by the government to poorer countries when there are natural disasters.

Education even at its highest level does not translate into professional positions with comparable incomes. Approximately 90% of the population works for the State and doctors get the same (modest) pay for brain surgery as they do for a sprained ankle. Thus, these highly skilled professionals make less than bartenders, cab drivers, and hotel maids who are able to accept tips from foreign visitors.

Employment and Entrepreneurship

Government-controlled employment has inspired citizens to turn to creativity, craftsmanship, and black or "gray" market dealings for extra income. An example is the repair and upkeep of the '50s cars and vehicles abandoned by Americans and defecting Cubans after the 1959 Revolution. Repairs and

 upgrades to the wonderful cars of the '50s—such as the CD player in Hemingway's car—come from ingenuity, improvising, and European parts since there has been an embargo on American parts for more than 50 years.

One of the highlights of my trip was the opportunity to ride in Hemingway's yellow, 1957 Pontiac convertible—with a CD player only playing Sinatra, a frequent Havana visitor.

Internet access and access to "capitalists" culture is severely limited by the government. Through various means, ambition, and skill, individuals have found a street-corner market by downloading TV programs, films, magazines, and music, then loading thumb drives and selling them for a few dollars. In our terminology, this creates a pyramid business. The variety of entrepreneurial ideas with minimal supplies is phenomenal.

Services are abundant. Tour guides and repair persons are readily available. But, visitors will not find an abundance of arts and crafts items to buy. After the revolution which "guaranteed" and forbade  individual ownership and selling, many of those craft skills were lost. It was refreshing to note that coached begging, common before the revolution, appears to be replaced with an energy to find a better way to improve economic status.

Lodging and Food Service

Hotels, built and managed by foreign corporations but majority-owned by the Cuban government, are modern and offer quality amenities. The popular trend is toward bed and breakfast service. Sufficient numbers of restaurants with broad menu selections are available offering quality food and excellent service.

Diners will find both the Continental and American style of dining etiquette with full awareness of proper settings and service. Most servers and hospitality  workers have good eye contact, and many speak both Spanish and English fluently, English being the international language.

Havana and the islands have a brisk tourist business from Europe and other countries not affected by the Cuba-American embargo.

Verbal and Non-verbal Language

Direct eye contact is common with most servers and citizens.

Handshakes are firm.

Non-verbal language positive.

Sights and Sounds

Music is happy. Flowers and shrubs are colorful. Beaches are clean and inviting. It should be noted on my visit the beaches were not available to Americans. Even today (2017), Americans are not allowed to visit as "tourists." Our country's embargo prohibits golf,

174

scuba diving, and other
leisure activities.

 **Dress**

Cubans dress well; no
sloppy or torn jeans and t-shirts!

Architecture (mostly Spanish Colonial) is outstanding
although many of the buildings are not yet back to their
former beauty. Construction, though on-going, is slow due
to the poverty in Cuba, and construction workers being
poorly paid government employees.

The marbled walkways on the plaza still offer another touch
of splendor.

Travel, lodging, and food are pricey.

Would I return? Should the opportunity present itself, "Yes."
The numerous photo ops are in themselves my call to
return. I shall never forget my fascinating visit to Cuba.

*__Jeanne Baer__ is an author, professional speaker, and
photographer. She's lived in five countries and traveled to
30, giving her ample opportunities to try to mind her
manners in several languages! Jeanne and her husband
live in Lincoln, Nebraska. You can reach her at her
Facebook page, Jeanne Baer Photos.*

Don't Forget Your Manners!
...On Public Transportation

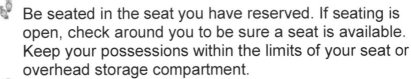

👣 Follow the rules as they apply to the mode of travel you have selected.

👣 Be seated in the seat you have reserved. If seating is open, check around you to be sure a seat is available. Keep your possessions within the limits of your seat or overhead storage compartment.

👣 Be mindful of the people seated around you. Some passengers come with planned work to accomplish; others come to have "down time" in their day; still others come looking for a conversation either with a "live" person or a lingering phone conversation. Let your wishes be known, in a respectful way of course.

👣 Don't put feet in the aisles or quickly push your seat back which could cause spills or cramps to those behind you.

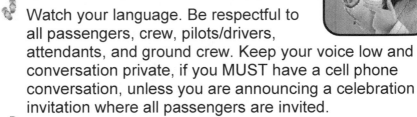

👣 Watch your language. Be respectful to all passengers, crew, pilots/drivers, attendants, and ground crew. Keep your voice low and conversation private, if you MUST have a cell phone conversation, unless you are announcing a celebration invitation where all passengers are invited.

👣 Deposit trash in trash containers.

👣 Push and shove have no place in public places: airports, terminals, stations, or parking lots. The more considerate the passengers, the easier the travel.

👣 Remember the tip for taxi drivers and porters—the more assistance they provide, the bigger the tip.

SMILE! Tired, happy, sad, relieved, or just glad to be on the "next step" of your journey. Allow others to begin their "next step" with a pleasant thought as well.

176

TRAVEL TO ISRAEL

*"Israel, a land of achievement and
discovery--where strawberries
bloom and cotton grows.
Israel, a nation of caring people
who respect their country and
their culture. Israel, my home."*

--Unknown

In my quest to bring listeners information on international travel and how to enjoy and respect different cultures, Israel was on my list. The order of achieving my goal was an opportunity. The opportunity came for a conversation with a native Memphian, my cousin, Gail Kirschner, who considers Israel her "second home" after 29 years' residence. Our conversation opened my eyes to the beauty and achievements of Israel, making it an attractive possibility for a travel destination.

Below are Gail's citizen-proud remarks on manners, customs, language, food, crafts, technology, and tourist "must see" spots in Israel, and in particular the area around Jerusalem.

Shalom, dear readers!

There is so much to share. Twenty-nine years ago, I must say arriving in Israel was a culture shock. Today, it is almost as natural as being in Memphis, Tennessee, United States of America.

 Primary Facts

Israel is the only state in the Middle East that is not Muslim. It is the only democracy. It is the center of the three major religions of the world.

 Language

Be comfortable knowing English will get you there! English is the primary language for most services: hotel, restaurant, shopping, transportation, and tourist attractions.

Greetings

Hold back on the American handshake until you see what the other person offers. Because of religious differences, men and women do not always share handshakes with the opposite gender.

Show a smile—this is always accepted. Offer a "Shalom"—meaning hello, goodbye, and a statement of peace. You are showing respect by your friendliness and acknowledgment of customs.

Time and Space

Recognize this is a fast-paced culture—in fact, almost aggressive at times.

Understand, no offense is intended with the closeness of people. They are just anxious to get their turn for service as quickly as possible.

Consider Edward T. Hall's four types of space. While Americans are more space conscious and cater to "social space" you might consider Israel more a "personal" space country.

Feel the pulse of the culture with the fast-paced walking habits.

Prepare for business to be conducted without the American "warm up" period.

Dress

Pack light and casual—unless you are invited to an event requiring a specific dress. This is a desert area: hot and dry.

Wear comfortable walking shoes. There is much to see and do involving walking and possibly hiking and climbing.

Keep your arms covered—no exception—in Jerusalem's religious sites.

Bring water shoes—not flip-flops— should you plan on visiting and entering the Dead Sea. The bottom is rocky and you don't want to cut your feet. Skip the need, gentlemen, to pack ties as they are seldom worn.

Shopping

Designer jewelry—especially silver— art, crafts, religious items, and body lotions from the Dead Sea are among the most popular.

Food

Hard to find "bad" food! Specialties: Falafel and Shwarma (lamb or turkey), pizza (thick crust) and sushi are favorites. Desserts are plentiful yet not "specialty items."

Both Kosher and Non-Kosher restaurants are easily found.

Hotels are known for breakfast buffets. Watermelon and cucumbers are favorite treats.

Favorite Tourist Sites

Suggest taking a tour or hiring a personal guide.

Visit and enjoy the many beaches.

Tour Western City Tunnel, under the remaining wall of the temple.

Visit the Dead Sea. Floating in the Dead Sea can be for fun, or for medicinal reasons, due to the high concentration of minerals.

This is near where the Dead Sea Scrolls were discovered. The Scrolls are now housed in the Israel Museum in Jerusalem.

Industry recognition shared with the world

Introduced Smartphone GPS system.

Recognized for high-tech expertise and development.

Known for medical and pharmaceutical discoveries and achievements.

Characteristics and manners of the Israeli people

Americans often view the Israeli as "rough around the edges" and aggressive.

Israeli people are caring to friend and stranger alike. They are ready to aid and guide wherever, whenever, and however needed.

Respect, for their surroundings and for the people, is evident and mutually appreciated.

An invitation is extended to each of you to visit and learn about Israel. Shalom!

Gail Sacks Kirschner immigrated to Israel with her husband and three children in 1987. They have lived in Maale Adumim, outside of Jerusalem, for almost all of these 30 years. She is presently the Administrative Coordinator for the Pardes Center for Jewish Educators at the Pardes Institute of Jewish Studies in Jerusalem.

Don't Forget Your Manners!
…With Your Business Card

🐾 Keep your business cards fresh and crisp--keeping them in a card case is a good idea.

🐾 Understand that the business card is recognized internationally, and the proper exchange of business cards is of professional importance.

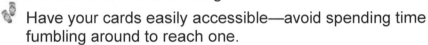

🐾 Exchange of business cards is usually done at the beginning or at the end of an initial meeting.

🐾 Have your cards easily accessible—avoid spending time fumbling around to reach one.

🐾 Hand your card so it is in reading position when received.

🐾 If contact information has changed, fix it before presenting your card—or no one can reach you. Then have new cards printed!

🐾 When receiving a business card, take a moment to look at it before putting it away.

🐾 Have one side of a business card printed in the language of the recipient when traveling internationally. Present the card with the recipient's language facing up.

🐾 Research how business cards are treated in different parts of the world before traveling. Local cultures vary.

LATIN AMERICAN TRAVEL

"The world is a book, and those who do not travel read only a page."
--Saint Augustine

Preparing for travel has never been easier. Searching the internet for entertainment, history, food, and lodging for your destination will provide you with a wealth of information.

Our conversations on my radio show also included etiquette and manners, both for business and pleasure—in the United States and beyond. It was my plan to explore the culture and customs of several countries and geographical areas on the weekly show. Dr. Lillian Chaney and I had conversations about international travel. She and I discussed an international travel checklist. She felt, and I agreed, it would be a great planning tool for any travel, particularly international.

We then decided to have other conversations on the show dealing with international destinations—time ran out! We had already prepared our outline for Latin America, and she graciously agreed to include it in the book. While you have this book in front of you, flip to the chapter, Checklist for International Travel—I think you will agree, by reviewing the topics, she has thought of almost everything you will need to investigate, review, and pack.

Dr. Lillian Hunt Chaney is the author of four books focusing on international and intercultural business communication and etiquette. In addition to holding the title Distinguished Professor of Office Management and Professor of Management at The University of Memphis, Memphis, Tennessee, U.S., for many years, she also taught at The University of San Andres in La Paz, Bolivia. She has made numerous visits to Mexico and Central America. Dr. Chaney shares comments today on selected Latin American countries with which U.S. companies conduct international trade. Included are Mexico, America's second largest export market, and selected countries of South and Central America.

The globalization of business has made it imperative that companies conducting business abroad arm themselves with the knowledge of the customs and manners of people of other countries. In addition, the U.S. workforce is becoming increasingly multiethnic, thus making it essential for U.S. workers to learn to understand people of other cultures to ensure successful interactions. They must realize what is acceptable behavior in the U.S. may be a serious mistake in another. We will follow our prepared checklist.

Greetings

- When interacting with people of other countries, making a faux pas when greeting others can be embarrassing. Greetings in the U.S. are highly ritualistic; they include a firm handshake accompanied by a verbal greeting of "How are you?" Latinos view this greeting exchange as insincere because people of the U.S. do not really want to know how you are.

- In Latin American countries, the handshake is also a proper greeting between people in business. However, more personal greetings include embracing and kissing, especially in Mexico, after you have established rapport. In Costa Rica, the greeting may be a handshake, as in the U.S., and accompanied by a verbal greeting, such as *Buenos dias* (good morning/day), *Buenas tardes* (good afternoon), or *Buenas noches* (good evening).

Introductions

- When making introductions in many Latin American countries, use the title with the surname. If you do not know the surname, use of only the title is acceptable: Señor, Señorita, Doctor (Ph.D. or physician) and Ingeniero (engineer). Surnames include the mother's maiden name: Teresa Gomez Sanchez is addressed Señorita Gomez. In Argentina, their unique naming conventions are different from many other Spanish-speaking cultures. Argentines use just one surname. Research that information before you travel.

Business Cards

- Business card exchange is important in Latin American countries. Have your business cards printed in English on one side and in Spanish on the other side (except in Brazil, where the information would be printed in Portuguese). Latinos place great importance on titles; be sure to include your title on your card, along with your rank, profession, degrees, phone numbers (with international codes), and your email address.

Verbal Communication

- Verbal or spoken communication includes small talk or chitchat—both U.S. persons and Latin Americans are very good at small talk. Topics for chitchat in Latin American countries include sports, the arts, local sights, history, and international travels. Be complimentary and noncritical. Slang expressions, such as ballpark figure (for estimate), should be avoided.

Conversational Taboos

- In Latin American countries, conversational taboos include politics, religion, economic problems, social class differences, and personal questions—which they may ask. Avoid anything that would cast their country in a negative light, such as recent disasters.

Humor

- U.S. presentations often start with a joke or cartoon to establish a relaxed atmosphere before getting down to business. In many countries, this is viewed as failing to take the business at hand seriously. Brazilians, for example, do not use humor during business meetings. If you do use humor, stick to what is considered acceptable international humor, which is slapstick, restaurant jokes, and humorous stories about golfers.

Dining Etiquette

- Many business and social encounters involve dining. It is important to be aware of cultural variations in eating styles and mealtime customs. In Latin American countries, the Continental eating style is used (the fork remains in the left hand, tines down, during cutting and eating the food).

- Leaving some food on your plate is expected in Costa Rica and Colombia, as is the practice in the U.S. It indicates that you had enough to eat. In Bolivia, Peru, and Panama, leaving food is viewed as wasteful. In the U.S. and in Latin American countries, making noises while eating is considered inappropriate. Sometimes it is best *not* to know what you are eating. Best advice—eat what you are served, pretend it is chicken, and swallow it quickly.

Tipping

- Tipping guidelines in South American countries and in the U.S. are quite similar—15-20% in restaurants; the tip is often included in the bill. In Mexico check to see that the amount added is the tip and not a tax.

- Because of the variations within the country, ask at your hotel what is customary.

Time

- The general rule to follow is to be on time or even a little early for meetings and appointments (except for social engagements when you are expected to arrive 30 minutes after the stated time). This is expected of international visitors although Latin Americans may be 15 minutes late.

- The concept of time when doing business in Mexico is not the same as in the U.S. For this reason, you may want to ask whether an appointment is *la hora Americano* (American time) or *la hora Mexicana* (Mexican time) where one would arrive 15 minutes to an hour after the scheduled time.

- Another point which has caused confusion to Latin American visitors is the use of the word mañana, which literally translated means tomorrow or morning. It can also mean later. When you are told the contract will be ready for signing mañana, it may not mean the next day.

Dress

- People form impressions of others based on their dress and appearance. Conservative business attire with a classic, traditional look and conservative accessories are highly recommended for conducting business in Latin America. In fact, what you wear and your credibility are linked; without a positive initial impression, you may not get a chance to show how competent or knowledgeable you are.

- Business casual attire is usually recommended for travel; however, some companies expect their employees to dress professionally when traveling on business. In Latin American countries, dress well and conservatively. Accessories, such as a leather briefcase, should be of high quality. In Mexico, do not wear shorts on the street or jeans or tennis shoes if you are on an official business trip. Mexican business people do not wear such casual attire.

Gestures

- No gestures have universal meanings across cultures; what is positive in one country may be insulting in another. For example, the OK sign, which is positive in the U.S., is obscene in Brazil; the vertical horns gesture, which has a positive meaning in the U.S., is obscene in Brazil. It is important to research gestures of the Latin American country you plan to visit—good advice may be to use few gestures.

Eye contact

- Direct eye contact is expected by people in the U.S. macroculture; differences exist in people of U.S. microcultures. Direct eye contact signifies that you are listening; it's a way of showing respect. However, prolonged eye contact may be viewed as threatening. In some Latin American cultures, prolonged eye contact is typical—try to follow the lead of your host. In some Latin American countries, status is a consideration in eye contact. For example, Latin Americans avoid direct eye contact when conversing with their supervisors to show respect. Mexico is a bit different from other Latin American countries regarding eye contact. When talking with a Mexican, break eye contact regularly.

Space and Touch

- U.S. persons need more space and do not touch as much as do Latin Americans. Americans prefer to stand about 4 to 12 feet apart when interacting in business situations and rarely touch except to shake hands. Latin Americans need less space and stand closer together when conversing. Touching arms and patting backs are very common in Mexico. After establishing rapport, expect an embrace when your Mexican host greets you.

Color

- Colors have special meanings in certain cultures. Blue is a safe color for marketing products as it is preferred by consumers in many countries. Red should be used with caution when marketing products internationally.

- Although a red circle on products sold in Latin American countries was successful, using red for packaging is not a good idea in some countries because of negative connotation associated with a country's flag or political beliefs.

- Certain types or colors of flowers have negative connotations and should be used with caution. Lilies are used by Mexicans to lift superstitious spells, and yellow flowers are associated with death. In Brazil, avoid wearing green and yellow. These are the colors of the Brazilian flag, and people of Brazil do not wear them.

Of course, there is much more to caution international travelers about; however, we had only an hour conversation! These tips will get you started. There is plenty of additional written information available through *Amazon.com* and on the internet as well.

Be a polished ambassador for your country.
Enjoy your adventure.

Dr. Lillian H. Chaney *was a Distinguished Professor of Office Management and Professor of Management at The University of Memphis, Memphis, Tennessee, for many years. She co-authored six books and over 100 articles in professional journals, in addition to conducting seminars for corporate and professional groups. Her awards include the University's Distinguished Teaching Award.*

Quiz 1 Answers
1. The magic words are: **b. Please and Thank You**
2. Where is the place for name tag? **b. On the right shoulder.**
3. When visiting for a job interview: **a. When invited to be seated and in the seating offered.**
4. What communication skill is most likely to prevent the most errors? **b. Listening.**
5. Which seat is designated as the place of honor at dinner? **a. The seat to the right side of the host/hostess.**

Quiz 2 Answers
1. Forks are on which side of the dinner plate? **b. Forks are on the left side of the dinner plate.**
2. What is the purpose of the two utensils at the top of your plate? **b. The two utensils are used for dessert.**
3. If your dinner partner asks for the pepper: **b. Pass the salt *and* pepper.**
4. Is it correct to cut your rolls? **a. No, you always break the rolls.**
5. After stirring your iced beverage: **b. Remove the spoon from the glass. Place it on the saucer under the glass but never on the tablecloth.**

Quiz 3 Answers
1. Should you need to leave the table during dinner, place napkin: **b. In the seat of your chair.**
2. If your napkin falls to the floor, you should: **b. Pick it up, if it is accessible, and ask the server for a clean one.**
3. When you have finished your meal, place your napkin: **a. Loosely folded and to the left of your dinner plate.**
4. Where do you place your cell phone on the table? **b. There is no place on the table for your cell phone.**
5. When you need to attract the attention of the server. **b. Catch eye contact or gently hold your hand just above the table.**

ON-THE-GO TIPS CARDS

For quick reference when you are on the go, take the
On-The-Go Tips card with you.

Just cut out the cards and take them with you.

If you have downloaded the electronic version of *MANNERS
ON THE MOVE*, follow the link to Manners Always Matter
website to download a pdf to print the On-The-Go Tips cards
whenever you want.

www.MannersAlwaysMatter.com
Click on "Tips Cards" and download the set.

Consider ordering a copy of the book
as a GIFT
to your favorite person, school, or organization

1. Dinner Plate 6. Salad Fork
2. Soup Bowl 7. Dinner Fork
3. Bread Plate 8. Butter Spreader
4. Salad Plate 9. Dessert Spoon
5. Napkin 10. Dessert Fork
11. Dinner Knife
12. Teaspoon
13. Soup Spoon
14. Iced Beverage Spoon
15. Water Glass
16. Red Wine Glass
17. White Wine Glass

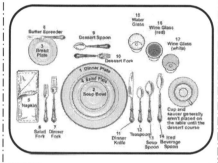

Don't Forget Your Manners in Languages

Language	Hello
Spanish	Hola
French	**Bonjour**
German	Hallo or Guten Tag
Italian	**Ciao**
Mandarin	Ni Hau
English	**Hello**
	(or in the South, Hey, y'all)

Four Steps to a
Proper Handshake

As you approach someone, extend your right arm when you are about three feet away. Slightly angle your arm across your chest, with your thumb pointing up.

Lock hands, thumb joint to thumb joint. Then, firmly clasp the other person's hand, without any bone crushing or macho posturing.

Pump the other person's hand two to three times.

Let go.

CAUGHT
IN THE ACT!

*Your manners
and/or etiquette
was noticed and
appreciated.*

Thank
You

Don't Forget Your Manners in Languages

Language	Please	Thank You
Spanish	Por favor	Gracias
French	S'il vous plait	**Merci**
German	Bitte	Danke
Italian	**Per favore**	**Grazie**
Mandarin	Qing	Xie xie
English	**Please** (or in the South, Thanks, y'all)	**Thank You**

Dining Etiquette Reminders

- Reply to invitations by date requested.
- Place napkin in lap; use only to pat mouth.
- Keep elbows off the table during meal.
- Remove spoon from cup/glass before drinking.
- Chew with mouth closed; don't overload mouth.
- Taste food before adding salt/pepper/etc.
- Break bread. Butter one piece at a time.
- Cut meat one or two bites at a time.
- Place utensils at 10:20 position when done.
- Place napkin to left of plate when done.
- Thank host/hostess before leaving.

Manners Always Matter

Manners Always Matter

from the sandbox to the executive suite

Dr. Janet T. Cherry
Communication and Etiquette Coach

901-682-1359
www.MannersAlwaysMatter.com
JanetCherry@MannersAlwaysMatter.com
janetcherrytrainer@gmail.com
405 S. Perkins #450, Memphis, TN 38117

A good handshake should be firm and held no more than three-to-four seconds. In our culture, eye contact accompanies the handshake.

Ladies, it is acceptable for you to make the first move.

If you are initiating a handshake and the person to whom you have extended your hand does not reciprocate, say nothing, and simply move your hand back.

An informal way to greet someone you know is a high five."

Another alternative is the "fist bump." Two people form right hands into a fist and gently bump one another's fist.

ACKNOWLEDGEMENTS

Many thanks to the following guests. Without their expert comments, this book would not have been possible.

Ali Agha, Dr. Lillian H. Chaney, Jim Frommel, Phyllis and Ella Gregory, Jimmy Hoxie, Evonne Siemer, and Grant Whittle, Memphis, TN. **Doris Shumaker,** Clarksville, TN. **Stephen Brittain (Britt) Thompson,** Oxford, MS.

Contact information for the other guests is listed below.

Dr. Barbara D. Davis, Associate Professor
Coordinator, Business Communication, Coordinator,
Business Etiquette, The University of Memphis
Fogelman College of Business and Economics
Management Department, Memphis, TN 38152
bddavis@memphis.edu

Jeanne Baer, *jbaerphotos@gmail.com*

Ann Marie Easton, Pawsitive Companionship LLC
www.pawscompanion.com

Gregory J. Griffin, Assistant Manager and Funeral Director,
Memorial Park Funeral Home and Cemetery
5668 Poplar Avenue, Memphis, TN 38119-0885
901-767-8930, *griffing@nsmg.com*

Anthony L. Holmes, Founder, UCanBe Movement
CEO, Reality Records, Producer, KWAM 990 FM Talk Radio
3757 Earls Court Rd., Memphis, TN 38118
888-252-0757, *UCanBeMovement@gmail.com*
http://www.realityrecordssite.com/ucanbe

Toni Johnson, *ToniCoach@aol.com*

Gail Kirschner, *Gail.kirschner@gmail.com*

Mario Lara, President, Wright Property Management
5050 Poplar Avenue, Suite #920, Memphis, TN 38157
901-327-7916, *mariolara@wrightpm.com*
www.wrightpm.com

Betsy Comella McKay, *betsy@saltstyleandevents.com*

Liz McKee, Director of Internal Communications
Baker, Donelson, Bearman, Caldwell & Berkowitz, PC
165 Madison Avenue, Suite 2000, Memphis, TN 38103
Direct: 901-577-8185, Fax: 901-577-0868
lmckee@bakerdonelson.com, www.bakerdonelson.com

Clare Novak, President, Novak and Associates
2602 Trinity Ct., Chester Springs, PA 19425
NovakAssoc@gmail.com

James (JJ) Palmer, *Phadreus360@gmail.com*

Dan Phillips, Producer, *Dan323phillips@yahoo.com*

Victor Robilio, Author, *victorrobilio@gmail.com*

Michael R. **Sondag,** *Msondag52@gmail.com*

Mary W. **Sharp,** *mwsharp@bellsouth.net*

Jake C. Thompson, High School/Recruiting
The Oxford Eagle, Supertalk North Mississippi
Oxford, MS 38655, *Jthomp10_528@msn.com*

Dr. Kathy Tuberville, *k.tuberville@memphis.edu*

Keith P. Wiley, Driving Instructor, Pitner Driving School, Inc.
1918 Exeter Rd., Suite #2, Germantown, TN 38138
901-767-4704, *pitnerdriving@comcast.net*
www.PitnerDriving.com

ABOUT THE AUTHORS

Dr. Janet T. Cherry, a native Memphian, is a certified etiquette coach with faculty experience in business communications at The University of Memphis. She is an author, frequent speaker, former small business owner, and corporate specialist in management training and development.

As a radio talk show host, she interviewed guests locally, nationally, and internationally whose broad knowledge of life's everyday occasions planted the seed for this book. Without exception, there was agreement of a growing lack of respect by individuals for themselves and others--a lack of manners. *Manners on the Move* addresses these common, everyday situations with quick and easy tips and shows how to move childhood play into the executive suite. If you have a need to know yet have limited time to learn, join other readers who have found answers within these pages.

JanetCherryTrainer@gmail.com

Judith A. Burda is a graphics design specialist with a background in education, photography, printing, and manuscript editing, as well as over 25 years in post-high school teaching, in the office environment as an accountant and marketing coordinator, and as a small business owner.

She and Dr. Cherry have worked together on a number of projects before collaborating on *Manners on the Move*. Judy excels in drawing the mind's eye to the message through her spot-on graphic interpretation of the written word. Her graphics shed lighthearted humor in serious observation of common, everyday faux pas of mannerisms considered as "polished presence" in our culture.

twburda@bellsouth.net

GRAPHIC COPYRIGHTS

Unless individually noted on this page, all other photographs were purchased from Adobe Stock.
Photographs of Dr. Janet T. Cherry, Judith A. Burda, illustrations, and vectors are the property of
Dr. Janet T. Cherry and Judith A. Burda

Cover

46607603. Copyright: <a href='http://www.123rf.com/profile_iconicbestiary'>iconicbestiary / 123RF Stock Photo</a>

36489290. Copyright: <a href='http://www.123rf.com/profilezhaconda'>zhaconda / 123RF Stock Photo</a>

17259482. Copyright: <a href='http://www.123rf.com/profile_print2d'>printed / 123RF Stock Photo</a>

Sand Castle: Image ID: 48889767 (XXL). Copyright: <a href='http://www.123rf.com/profile_iimages'>iimages / 123RF Stock Photo</a>

Formal Dining Picture (page 80)

<a href="https://openclipart.org/pdf/181486/Cake.pdf">Cake (PDF)</a>

Workplace Manners and Internal Communication (page 61)

Quote by Paul J. Meyer: Permission granted by The Meyer Resource Group,® Inc. All rights reserved.

Thank You (Page 27)

Thank you notes: Phyllis and Ella Gregory

GUEST INDEX

Agha, Ali 47
Baer, Jeanne 171
Chaney, Dr. Lillian H. 165
Chaney, Dr. Lillian H. 183
Davis, Dr. Barbara D. 13
Easton, Ann Marie 115
Frommel, Jim 17
Griffin, Gregory J. 141
Holmes, Anthony "Dulaa" 25
Hoxie, Jimmy 109
Johnson, Toni 39
Johnson, Toni 43
Kirschner, Gail Sacks 177
Lara, Mario 135
McKay, Betsy Comella 145
McKee, Elizabeth 61
Novak, Clare 55
Palmer, James (JJ) 95
Phillips, Dan 123
Pokrandt, Agnes M. 67
Robilio, Victor 91
Sharp, Mary 149
Shumaker, Doris 103
Siemer, Evonne T. 75
Sondag, Michael R. 51
Thompson, Jake C. 131
Thompson, Stephen B. (Britt) 99
Tuberville, Dr. Kathy 4
Whittle, F. Grant 109
Wiley, Keith 153

Don't Forget Your Manners!
...Anywhere and Everywhere

American Flag — Thoughtfulness

Worship — hospitality — Cell Phone — Raining — Please — success — Listening — Sports — Dining — Excuse Me — Gay — Impressions — Questioning — Funeral — kindness — Ladd — SCHOOL — Snowing — Travel — Wine — Thank You — SERVERS — RSVP — Manners — LANGUAGES — DRIVING — Restroom — sales — sidewalks — Pop-up — Dress — Streets — friend — Cub — love — Israel — Sandbox — Grocery — CONDOMONIUM — roommates — Gentleman — smile — escalator — Theatre — communication — Buffet — dogs — Compliment — INTERVIEWS — Break-Up — Conversations

Any following pages are intended to be blank.

Made in United States
Orlando, FL
05 November 2023

38605753R00111